To Tress;
with love
Brian

A MESSAGE FOR ITS OWN TIME

May the Holy Spirit
touch your hearts
as you read this book

Anne

By Fr Brian Murphy

And

Anne Bardell B.Div., M. Ed., Lic. Div. (Cat)

Grosvenor House
Publishing Limited

This book is published by
Grosvenor House Publishing Ltd
Link House
140 The Broadway, Tolworth, Surrey, KT6 7HT.
www.grosvenorhousepublishing.co.uk

A CIP record for this book
is available from the British Library

ISBN 978-1-80381-390-5

DEDICATION

To all who have been our teachers beginning with our parents and including those we have had the privilege of working with over many years in our parishes.

With gratitude to all the friends and relatives who have supported us through reading the many draft copies of this book and offering invaluable comments.

CONTENTS

SECTION II - THE GOOD NEWS

SECTION III - EVER OLD AND
EVER NEW

SECTION IV- PRACTICAL CONSIDERATIONS
FOR PARISH ADULT CATECHETICS

PREFACE

Most of this book is written by myself, Fr. Brian Murphy, a priest in the Diocese of Salford in the north west of England. I have been a priest there for over 53 years with 33 of those years as parish priest in Salford and latterly in Lancashire. I am now retired. Early on, I helped organised the Charismatic renewal in the north west of England, and have always tried to look ahead to the future of the Church.

It has been written in collaboration with Anne Bardell a true lover of the Church whom I met over forty years ago. When I became Parish Priest in 1987, I asked her to come and work with me as Pastoral Assistant, she left a good teaching career to work for the Church. We have acted as a team since then in two parishes for over 32 years. She shares the views expressed in this book. It is a collaboration of us both, and the final section is written by her.

We have been inspired by the hopeful words of St John Henry Newman one and a half centuries ago,

> *'What I desire in Catholics is the gift of bringing out what their religion is. I want a laity, not arrogant, not rash in speech, not disputatious, but people who know their religion ... who enter into it, who know their creed so well that they can give*

an account of it, who know so much of history that they can defend it.'[1]

Throughout the years we have tried to find ways to bring people to realise that Jesus wants an individual relationship with each of us where he can teach us about his Father's love. Increasingly, we have witnessed people's hearts starting to burn within them when they begin to understand their growing relationship with Jesus and their role in his Church. We have found people of every age asking 'why did we not hear this before?' and have seen people from every walk of life, with their own skills and stories, awakening to the depth of their calling to share in the Royal Priesthood of Christ.

Through different approaches, we have found among numerous Church-going Catholics the hunger to explore their faith in greater depth. We have witnessed them grow familiar with the story of Christ and his people. This inspires them with the confidence to pass it on to their peers and the next generation. We hope that, in some way, this book enables more people to know and share their faith more deeply.

At the same time, many concerned Catholic friends are asking what the Lord is doing in our time. In this book we attempt to share our vision of how, in this special time, Jesus is giving his Church a new and beautiful beginning, hence the title of this book.

---

[1] J. H. Newman 1851 *Lectures on the Present Position of Catholics (Works of Cardinal John Henry Newman: The Birmingham Oratory Millennium Edition S.)* (Leominster, Gracewing 2000)

SECTION I

THE THIRD AGE OF
THE CHURCH

Chapter 1

I AM GOING TO LEAD HER OUT INTO THE WILDERNESS AND SPEAK TO HER HEART[2]

The third phase of Christianity

In the past fifty years, people's lives have changed beyond recognition. Science has wonderfully transformed our potential, but its method of arriving at truth has increasingly become the 'only' way to know truth. The result is that many of the old certainties and perceptions have been labelled as myths. Today people wonder if anything is certain as different versions of truth claim attention. In the confusion many stop thinking deeply and instead concentrate on seeking enjoyment and prosperity.

The enjoyment industry, or leisure, has exploded. There are so many possible ways of having fun. The Cultural Revolution has changed the way we live, but we are more and more aware of mental sickness and sense that society is insecure. Fun seeking is taken as good, but research reveals that real happiness has been decreasing.

---

[2] Hos 2: 14

Prosperity has seemed achievable as never before. The world has been developing at a rapid pace, but some have enjoyed the increasing prosperity much more than others. This inequality has been exacerbated by the growth of the philosophy of individualism, the justification of greed, and the claims of entitlement. Due to the communications explosion it has become a much smaller world, and the differences in peoples' lives have been exposed. While some enjoy the 'good life', there is an increasing sense of wrong. Social unrest is growing.

Also, it is dawning on us that the earth's resources are limited and constant growth is not possible. Various ways forward are promoted, but people doubt that humanity has the good will to respond to the complex problems that face us. In an age when methodical scepticism has produced scientific wonders, there is a growing scepticism about our human future. Hope is in short supply.

Yet people want to hope. The Covid pandemic has made people think. We have seen graphically how our world is interconnected. We have celebrated those in society who serve the community often on meagre wages. Complacency is less prevalent and there is some evidence that a more thoughtful time may come. Hope is desired, but that can only spring from a vision of the future which is attractive and also attainable.

In the midst of all this change, Christianity, far from offering an inspiring vision, has seemed to fail in parts of the world which used to be called Christian, and many proclaim that we are now in a post-Christian age. This causes great distress to many of us, but I believe that we are really seeing the dawning glimmer of a new age of Christianity. Our Saviour is as busy as ever and he alone offers true hope to the world. The Church has been through different times and seasons in the past, and I am sure that God has brought us to the beginning of a new phase – a phase offering great hope to humanity. I shall try to give my rationale for my belief. It begins by going back in Church history and looking at the different phases so far.

The transition from the first to the second phase of the Church

In 313 AD, the Edict of Milan proclaimed tolerance of Christianity in the Roman Empire. During the previous three centuries, as the Church had spread across most of the Empire, it had endured a succession of vicious persecutions. Despite that, admiration and respect for its members had grown. Now, the Emperor Constantine was actively favouring the Church which he eventually joined. He supported the Church financially, built basilicas, granted privileges to clergy (such as exemption from certain taxes), promoted Christians to high office, and returned property confiscated during the long periods of persecution. From that time on, Christianity gradually became the religion of the Roman Empire. This brought to an end the first phase of Christianity which had begun with the Apostles, in which it had been a minority religion, gradually building a reputation for goodness and truth because of the dedication and virtue of its members, many of whom had undergone heroic martyrdom.

In this second phase of the Church, the majority of the population joined the Church, but they often did so for reason of advancement in the secular world, or because they followed their ruler. These motives did not involve a conversion of heart to the Lord. So the fervour and dedication of members of the Church became diluted, although there were still many holy and virtuous members. The second phase lasted into our own time.

Sixty years ago, being British was generally thought the same as being Christian. Laws and customs had grown out of Christian understanding, and to varying degrees, Church leaders enjoyed great respect. It was more or less similar in most of Europe and America, and much of Africa and Asia was rapidly becoming 'Christianised'. Since then things have changed greatly.

The second phase of the Church

In this second phase of the Church, (seventeen centuries long) Christians led great movements for the good of humanity. Examples of this are: the Benedictines helped settle much of Europe into agricultural civilisation, the Church founded the first hospitals and universities, and, in recent centuries it pioneered universal education. Many Saints shone with the life of the Spirit and gave inspiration which others followed; even the frequent wars were often tempered by Church attempts at peace-making and calls for justice; recently, the Church has spearheaded the roll-out of Covid vaccines in Amazonia.

There were also abuses and atrocities committed by Christians. Religious wars raged; in the crusades Catholics ransacked many Orthodox holy sites; genocide was rampant in the conquest and Christianisation of South America; and heretics were tortured and burnt, to name but a few scandalous episodes. Much of the corruption sprang from the assumption that it is right to work through the exercise of civil power. The love of power, politics and fanaticism constantly bedevilled the work of the Holy Spirit. If anyone wants to denounce Christianity, they will find plenty of instances of its failure. But the overall picture is one of great goodness and its being an enormous force for human progress. This is a thumbnail sketch of 1700 years of the Church's history, but it is an accurate description of how the Church has worked in its second phase.

Did the Church get it wrong?

With hindsight, we can attempt to find patterns in the history of this period which have brought us to the position where the Church in the west seems weak. This is especially so as we face the challenges of a culture which has rapidly moved away from the Church. In our rational age it is normal to analyse in intellectual ways, but Christians go deeper; they turn to the Holy Spirit and discern. We need to appreciate what our Father has been doing in the past centuries, and, since it seems he is now altering the paradigm, we must ask what is his intention for his Church now and in the future. To hear the Father's answer we need to listen carefully to the Holy Spirit.

It is important not to condemn Christians in past ages. We would not be where we are today if they had not lived lives of seeking God's will according to the lights they had at the time. Humanity develops, and what is obvious to us now was often not obvious to our ancestors. But above all, we Christians believe that God is the Lord of history and that, while he allows human beings freedom to choose good or evil, human actions can never cancel his plan. He can and does lead all things to the fulfilment of his ultimate goal, which is to bring mankind and all creation to the *'glorious liberty of the children of God'.*[3]

It is important to bear in mind that the Father develops his plan patiently. With myriad graces at every minute, and over many years, he inspires human beings to conversion of heart. He cooperates with people's many acts of love and courage and insight, and he foils many human excesses. And he leads us gently towards the restoring of all things in the new humanity, the Mystical Body of his Son.

God works gradually

Look at how the Spirit leads us. Take for example the way the Apostles seemed to accept slavery and the inequality of the sexes. St Peter (1 Pt 2: 18 ff) urges

---

[3] Rom 8: 21

slaves to be obedient to their masters, even to the extent of accepting harshness following the example of Christ's suffering for the sake of sinners. He urges wives to obey their husbands so that, through long-suffering and love, they might bring them to conversion.[4] Yet at the same time God through the Apostles is laying the seeds of slavery's abolition when Peter asserts in the same letter that none of us are slaves except to Christ since we have received the freedom of God's children. Slaves lost their identity and rights in Roman law so it was a shocking notion to the people of his time to say that slaves have dignity and an identity of the highest order.

Also, St. Paul sends the escaped slave Onesimus back to his master Philemon,[5] urging the latter to treat Onesimus as his '*brother*' – again a revolutionary concept. In his same first letter, Peter lays out the novel principle of wives' sexual equality to husbands, saying that they should '*respect their wives*' because '*she is equally an heir in the life of grace*'.[6] In Galatians, Paul[7] teaches radically that there is '*no difference between male and female*', '*all are one in Christ*'. It is difficult for us today to realise how revolutionary these teachings were. Because of them, over centuries, abusive practices which were woven unchallenged into the fabric of human society have been altered. Seeds laid by Christ into the human consciousness through the apostles have germinated, causing real change.

---

[4] 1 Pet 3: 1

[5] Phlm1:13

[6] 1 Pt 3: 7

[7] Gal 3: 25

The word of God usually acts as seeds laid in human souls working in hidden and gradual ways. This gives us an indication of how God is leading his Church of today into the future. Peter and Paul did not set out to abolish the Roman economic system (which depended heavily on slavery) nor to rewrite the contemporary laws on marriage. Economic systems and laws are for civil society to work on and improve over time. The mission of the Church, however, is to bring individuals and communities to the liberation of being followers of Christ. In that way, they will enable Christ to work through them with small and numerous graces to influence civil society's improvement. If there is one fault which characterises the second phase of Christianity, it is that Church members sought to use human influence, often force, to reshape society instead of leaving God time to take the initiative.

That has led to civil society reclaiming its proper authority often with strong suspicion of Church machinations. Forcing people to be good is not Christ's way, nor should it be the way of his people. Christ's way is to humbly take the sins of others on himself and lovingly serve them, firmly expecting that the Father's grace will bring about change in his brothers and sisters. Acting in the same way as Christ is the optimum option for Christians, because it produces results in the Father's timing, which is much quicker than human attempts at progress through polarisation and conflict. We may agonise over things that our contemporaries are doing, but using human force to correct situations will only make them worse. Using prayer and loving witness, trusting in the Father's power to affect change through grace, ultimately changes everything.

The third phase of the Church

It is my belief that we are entering a third phase of the Church's story, and that it is a natural progression in God's plan for mankind. It is a new beginning which can only start with deepening our knowing of Christ. Then we have to be honest; Cultural Catholics, pick-and-mix Catholics, Catholics who do not know Jesus cannot set the tone, agenda, nor future course of the Church. Neither can we attempt to accommodate these visions which we know to be impaired into the vision we are asking the Father to reveal to us. They are our family and, as in all true families, the weakest members need the greatest care and love. We must firmly resist their weakening of Christ's Church, but love them with great and tender love; they are good people, lovely people, and we must strenuously avoid any semblance of rejection, yet speak truth with heartfelt love.

One clear example is Baptism, which is the beginning of life with Christ. It should no longer be given because grandma has a fear of a child being excluded from heaven, or because parents desire a Catholic education for their children, or because clerics desire growth in Church membership numbers.

If parents have no connection to Christ other than a more or less fond attachment formed but not developed in their own childhood, they will not be able to lead their children into faith in Christ, since they do not experience it themselves. We must offer all parents appropriate opportunities to renew their own faith, before baptising their children and entrusting the new life in Christ to their care. Appropriate help calls for great inventiveness and guidance from God; it must be a real and positive invitation, not argumentative nor crushing the bruised reed with excessive demands. And we must make every effort to keep in contact with those who do not feel ready yet to take that step. Their hesitation is often because they are stressed and have heavy obligations working against their giving time to seeking Christ. This calls for great love and understanding and accompanying on behalf of pastors and helpers, certainly not rejection or condemnation. All we have to offer is affirmation, encouragement and the call to the supreme blessing of life in Christ. In the part of the Church where I am a priest we need to discuss who should be admitted to infant baptism and how the newly baptised are to be cared for. That would be one step among many towards bring us nearer to the fulfilling of the Father's plan for his Church in its third phase.

Likewise, the programmes for the Initiation of Adults needs to be reviewed. In the two parishes we have served, we have received many people into the Church, who, on reflection, seem to have entered for a sense of community and direction, rather than an encounter with Christ; so, many of them lapsed eventually. It is imperative that we acknowledge what is not working any longer, and be prepared to set out to where new and effective ways of fulfilling our mission lie. It is evident that the Father is shaking his Church to its foundations, but that is so that he can reveal the foundations anew.

It is like one of Giovanni Guareschi's Don Camillo stories,[8] which tells of the accidental breaking of a plaster statue of Our Lady in Church. It had always seemed crude and amateur; now they discovered that it had a much more beautiful and ancient statue of gold hidden within. It had obviously been hidden in that way to preserve it from some past threat of invasion. Its rediscovery brought great joy and an increase of devotion.

God is leading his Church into the desert to speak to her heart

In the third phase of the Church which is emerging, we are being stripped of our power, and deprived of the mind-set which claims the right to manipulate the city of this world into the city of God. Over the centuries of this second phase of the Church, which is now disappearing, humanity has passed through the rule of despots to tribally bonded societies to individualistic claims to independence. The Church has often attempted to harness these ways in which society worked. At other times, it has been a sign of contradiction. But all too often the Church has been reacting to the world it found itself in. Now we are being led to be proactive.

---

[8] G. Guareschi (1954) *The Ugly Madonna* in Don Camillos' Dilemma. (Wordpress [online] 2017)

Suddenly, and somewhat bafflingly, the Father is leading his Church into the wilderness. In stripping us of worldly power he is giving us no option but to kneel before him in the primary attitude of humanity before God. That is humility which owns its weakness and vulnerability, but is filled with overpowering hope and awareness that God is directing the course of history. We are brought to the point of seeking his guidance. As Jesus was led into the desert to be tempted, we are led to a desert experience to face truth and receive deep love and nourishment. As Jesus emerged from the desert spiritually empowered to bring salvation, so will we.

The Father has such a wondrous wish to renew and restore his beloved humanity; he will not be denied. He is calling his Church once more into the wilderness that lies in the hearts of all human beings so that he can restore our hearts with the ancient songs of his love. Some of our institutions and practices will go; some will be renewed; new ones will emerge. But they will only be effective if they proceed from his Spirit. He is urgent to renew the face of the earth: to bring about a fresh coming of the children of God to liberate creation, which is so longing for our touch.

God wishes his love affair with humanity to overflow the dams. St John Henry Newman chose as his motto 'heart speaks to heart'.[9] God opened his heart

---

[9] Newman's motto on his coat of arms when he was created a Cardinal J. H. Newman *Cor ad cor loquitur* The International Centre of Newman Friends [online]

totally to humanity when the Word became flesh. The children God loves will only arise afresh if, allowing him to speak to their hearts, they walk more closely with the one who called the fishermen on the lake of Galilee, know him intimately and learn from him who is meek and humble of heart.

Chapter 2

EVERYTHING FLOWS FROM A CLOSE FRIENDSHIP WITH JESUS

Jesus longs for friendship with you

Many of the good people I have served in parishes have told me that they pray to God, but, when we dig deeper, their prayer is mainly striving to do his will and be morally good, asking a lot for help, and, less frequently, giving thanks - praise is particularly difficult and often mechanical. Some have told me that they pray to Our Lady, and that they feel her motherly care for them, but their feelings for Jesus are mainly venerating him at a distance as God and trying to imitate him as a human being. For many, a close friendship with Jesus frequently sounds alien. These are good people who are living good lives, but the fact remains that they need more. They need Jesus' close friendship.

Also, amazingly, Jesus needs close friendship with each of us. Read these intense words of his from the Last Supper as he pours out his heart to his disciples:

*'I will not leave you orphans
I will come back to you
In a short time the world will no longer see me;
But you will see me'.* [10]

*'If anyone loves me he will keep my word,
and my Father will love him,
and we shall come to him
and make our home with him'.* [11]

In Revelations, the last book of the Bible, Jesus says:

*'Look, I am standing at the door, knocking.
If one of you hears me calling and opens the
door, I will come in to share his meal, side by side
with him'.* [12]

These are words of a close and very intimate friend. In the last chapter of St John's Gospel, Jesus takes aside Peter, who is consumed with self-hatred because he has deserted and rejected Jesus publicly three times. Jesus simply asks him *'Do you love me?'* [13] three times. These are not the words of a distant God, but one who loves us so much that he comes among us and calls each one of us to friendship.

Friendship starts when we move from knowing about someone to knowing and caring for them

---

[10] Jn 14: 18-19

[11] Jn 14: 23

[12] Rev 3:20

[13] Jn 21: 15 ff

intimately. It is a movement from the head to the heart. Once a person is in your heart, they have some control over your happiness. If you love someone with all your heart, you give them utter control. Jesus asks you to give him just that, which frightens most of us, because we have to trust big time. We have been wounded by others so many times in our lives that we wrap a shield around ourselves and find it very hard to let anyone else in. Believing in someone is difficult. Yet many times in the Gospels, Jesus asks people who are requesting a cure '*do you believe?*'[14]

'*Only have faith*'[15]

What did this puzzling question mean? It certainly did not mean 'do you believe I am the Son of God become flesh in order to redeem the human race?' It was only after the resurrection that they began to realise that this was the case. What did he mean then? He was asking them to open their hearts to God, even though they found that challenging. Basically, Jesus was asking them to step out of their usual thought processes by which they normally made sense of the world and felt that they had some control, and instead, to give the initiative to God. He wants them to begin to say 'I am in your hands'. He knew that the cure they asked for was dependant on their surrender to God, even if it was a weak surrender, like the father of the

---

[14] Jn 9:35; Mt 9: 28
[15] For example Mk 5: 37

sick child who replied: *'Lord, I believe. Help my unbelief'.*[16]

Each time we open and give our hearts to God, we allow him to act in gracious and wonderful ways. It is the heart that matters. Many people believe that Jesus is the Word made flesh, but only with their heads. What he wants is that we give him our hearts, because it is all about love. As our intimacy with Jesus deepens we become more like him and we take our place more surely in God's restoration of the face of the earth.[17]

In the Gospels, Jesus never required his disciples to accept formulas summarising the truths about God. These dogmas were gradually defined over centuries because lovers of Jesus wanted to know more surely the truth about him in order to know him better personally. They wanted to walk with him like the disciples travelling to Emmaus. They wanted to find their hearts *'burning within'* them as he explains the scriptures to them.[18] He could have sent those disciples a long letter giving the same teaching, but it was in the encounter with the stranger, the fellow traveller, that the Emmaus walkers came alive. He not only imparted knowledge, but he gave love, skilfully working on their hearts not just their minds. He gave encouragement and personal attention, moving them to wonder. This

---

[16] Mk 9: 25
[17] Ps 104: 30
[18] Lk 24: 32

wonder caused them to urge him to stay the night and finally to recognise him *'at the breaking of bread'*.[19]

Jesus walks, often unrecognised, with you and me, but he wants us to recognise him and be in love with him. He is calling, but we will not hear unless we reach the point of seeking him. The two Emmaus disciples had known Jesus, perhaps for years, but it was only when they thought they had lost him that they yearned for him. Their hearts were ready to open to his deep and personal love. Each of us needs to yearn to know him personally.

There comes a moment when we invite him into our hearts for the first time. He will always respond. He yearns for us much more than we yearn for him. Once he has come through the door of our hearts the relationship will develop. Sometimes he will seem to withdraw, but that is to invite you to seek him even more deeply. Sometimes he will speak words into your mind. Much of the time, you will find him quietly inspiring you as you ponder the events of your life and ask for his guidance. You will also be led into the mystery of his divinity, which transcends our capacity to know. Then the response is stillness, wonder, worship and awe – sometimes fear.

None of us is truly religious if we only know about God and do not have a personal relationship with Jesus. God will never be satisfied with any relationship with us except love. There is no escaping the fact that close

---

[19] Lk 24: 35

friendship with Jesus is necessary for a full Christian life. That is because Christian life is about being incorporated into the Trinity, and Trinity life consists entirely of personal relationships. As the Holy Spirit's action within us grows, we realise more and more that the Father offers us nothing less than a personal loving closeness through Jesus. Jesus is the face that God presents to us. This earth was made so that we human beings can have and live Trinity life, and lead all creation into the heavenly love affair.

The mystery is Christ among you, your hope of glory[20]

We Catholics do not stress relationship with Jesus as the basic root of Christianity in isolation. We express it more radically: **a relationship with Jesus in his body, his Church.** The power of the Church proceeds only from the fact that it is the Body of Christ. The dynamism of the Church proceeds only from the Holy Spirit. Christ has entered our world first in a physical body, and then in a spiritual, mystical body whereby his Spirit draws individuals into himself in a way that we gradually act more from his person living in us than from our own initiative.[21] That does not destroy our own individuality but matures it, because our full identity was always intended to arise from our bond with God. Likewise, as his Spirit draws many individuals in the same way into Christ, his one Spirit

---

[20] Col 1: 27
[21] Gal 2: 20

draws them all into communion. We become bonded as brothers and sisters and are formed into one body.

All of this is a mystical reality which does not mean that it is unreal, but that it happens on a far deeper level than the material world which we grasp with our senses, or the emotional world which we feel, or the intellectual level which knows through ideas. Our spirits are deeper than any of these levels; they are the heart of each one of us where we relate to God. Since the fall of mankind, our spirits have been in a coma-like state. Just as relatives and carers will speak to someone in a coma believing that, on a deep level, they might be heard, God speaks into the heart of each person. It is our woundedness which inhibits us from hearing clearly, and yet deep down in each of us there is a restlessness which aches for the divine.

Some people have decided that there is no God, but most are more accurately described as agnostic. They can't say they know God and they can't say they don't. It is an ache which will not go away. The good news of Christianity proclaims that God has begun the awakening of humanity by becoming flesh as Jesus, the Son of God and the Son of Man. He has the unique power to operate in the heart of each of us, because he has drawn the heart of each and all of us into his own as he hung on the cross. There, he cleansed and renewed all hearts by taking them to his Father in heaven, even as the weight and experience of all broken hearts caused him unimaginable suffering. Now he enters into each heart that will open to him and involves them in the restoration of humanity. This Jesus event is the cataclysmic revival of humanity.

Now, as the Spirit lifts people into deep personal relationship with Jesus, men and women begin to live the life of God. We are like Lazarus called back from the dead. We emerge bound and wrapped in darkness and he commands: *'unbind him/her and let him/her go free!'*[22]

The Spirit of God is not material, or a feeling or an idea, but it is known by its fruits. His deep activity in our spirits produces effects in our material, emotional and rational faculties. Sometimes we feel wonderful peace, sometimes deep need, sometimes we receive an intuition or realisation, sometimes mountains move mysteriously. There is something happening to us deep inside, which we respond to with increasing trust and it is transforming us. After our leaving this world, it is the spiritual which will be most clearly experienced, and the material, emotional and rational universe will be completely realigned.

Eventually, at his Second Coming, space and time will be changed and the wedding of Christ and humanity will become gloriously complete. But there is a process of humanity's gradual progression to that completion, which we call Church, the gradual growth of the mystical body of Christ in space and time. Every man, woman and child is intimately involved, because all, deep down are part of the awakening, and Christ is calling all mankind to life. His Spirit draws people more and more into conscious and voluntary membership of his Body.

---

[22] Jn 11: 44

Chapter 3

OUR ORIGINS

One of things that puts people off talking about a close friendship with Jesus is that it sometimes sounds as though it is all about our feelings and our consolation. It will seem very self-centred if it is divorced from the reality of our need to seriously cooperate with him in the demanding work of salvation.

Today, while evil comes to meet us at every turn, there is an industrial-scale denial that we share responsibility for it. All sorts of excuses are offered to bolster the belief that we are the victims of evil forces within and without. It is as though we hardly have any free will, and therefore little responsibility. Christianity firmly holds that we are free beings; that all of us sin and must own our individual and shared responsibility for evil, and that we must freely participate in the work of restoring human holiness. We base this belief on the teaching at the beginning of the Bible.

But there we have a problem because many modern people rightly do not believe that the Bible's accounts of creation and the beginning of the human race with Adam and Eve are strict history. We Christians, who base our understanding of God and mankind on them, have been slow to perceive how many people are put off by the way we talk about these stories. We have to help people to understand the origin and meaning of the beginning of the Bible.

In modern times, there have been huge developments in our knowledge of history. In the past century, it has revealed more and more of how people have acted and developed over the ages. History necessarily concentrates on the millennia for which we have written records. Archaeology adds to our understanding. It tells us a great deal as more and more traces of early peoples and civilisations are unearthed. Timescales of human developments have become more clear. Yet, despite the endless research, there is no evidence in science of how humanity started.

We Christians pose the question of how humanity started in these terms: when did the human soul begin? The soul is the source of our capacity to reflect on ourselves and to take conscious decisions to alter our behaviour rather than be driven by our basic instincts. We could put it another way: when did we begin to love using our free will? The answer we believe that God has given us is contained in the stories of Adam and Eve and all Christianity's understanding stems from there.

It is not strict history; but instead the stories illustrate the answers to two elementary factors at play in our world. The first is the age-old questioning of why we are here and how we find happiness. The second is the process by which the Creator has communicated with us, and how he has unveiled himself to us.

The quest to discover why are we here and how we achieve happiness

Modern interest in our family trees is evidence of how we feel the need to understand our origins in order to gain some understanding of who we are. Since we are not privy to the details of remote history we have to use our imaginations and intelligence to construct explanations of how the traditions and religions developed in different peoples as they sought to give answers to these basic questions.

The ancient peoples did not have books or computers, they had stories which they told round the campfires in the quiet of the night. The story tellers were remarkable for their retentive memories and what was passed down varied little over the generations. Where it did develop was where sages added details to introduce deeper meaning. The traditions of different people became established and were accepted into the communal understanding of the family, the tribe and eventually nations.

Many of these accounts from the different traditions have survived and they show great similarities. They usually agree on the creation of humanity by divine beings. These were very human-like, but with super powers. They were given characteristics like violence, selfishness, lust, devotion and vulnerability. Whenever we seek to explain something, we will do so in terms with which we are familiar. So the gods of myth were created in our own image. Since these primitive religions were mostly modelled on ourselves, they did little to shed light on why we are here and where happiness lies.

How the Creator reveals himself to us

All of this is a proper subject for scientific consideration. But the power of science to supply answers ends at the frontier of human intuition and belief. Here explanations of our origin and happiness can only be tested by the effects they have over time, and competing religions are judged by their fruits.

At a non-Christian funeral recently, the last song had these words: '*I don't believe in an interventionist God*',[23] but the chorus was a plea to 'Dear Lord'. It offered no answers, but it expressed the anguished human quest to know the answers to the age-old questions. We Christians definitely believe in an interventionist God. More than that, we believe that God has gradually revealed himself to humanity over the centuries until the fullness of his self-revelation came when his Son, his Word, his full expression of himself, became human as Christ. Christ then appointed messengers, or apostles whom he had taught and whom he commissioned to hand on the completed revelation that the God who reveals himself in Christ is family, love and goodness, and we are his children.

Where does Adam and Eve come into all this? In the midst of myths about competing gods, there appeared a tale of a good, holy God who made us well in his own

---

[23] 'I don't believe in an interventionist God' by Nick Cave

image. The pervasive experience of evil was explained by an account of the first human beings choosing to know evil and bringing disaster into the world. The disaster was not to last for ever, but evil would be crushed by an *'offspring'* of *'the Woman'*.[24] We believe that, in his careful planning, God inspired the sages who elaborated this tradition. The next big step of his self-revelation was to form a close relationship with one of the ancients whom he gifted with enormous faith. His name was Abraham, and God ensured that Abraham's family adhered to the story of Adam and Eve.

They did not have our strict method of verifying history and they even saw no contradiction in holding to the two differing accounts of creation in chapters 1 and 2 of Genesis. In the first chapter, God made man and woman on the sixth day after creating all the other plant and animal life on earth. In the second account in chapter 2, he made the man first then created plants and animals to provide him with companionship, but they did not satisfy him. God finally created woman and the man's happiness was complete. Having two contradictory stories did not bother previous generations, but simply explained different aspects of what God was revealing.

As the family of Abraham developed into the nation of Israel, they learned to write, and gathered their stories into books. These were eventually compiled into the Old Testament as we know it. The process of compilation was completed only a few decades before

---

[24] Gen 3: 15

Jesus was born. The Jews accepted the authority of the compilers. They and we believe that God inspired these compilers to select the writings which contained the truth about him, and to reject those which did not. Even then, there were two compilations of texts, one in Hebrew by the religious authorities in Jerusalem, the other in Greek by the renowned Jewish school of Alexandria in Egypt which accepted seven more books as inspired by God. This latter version was used by the vast majority of Jews who in fact were living all over the world outside Israel where Greek was the common language, like English is today.

Most people over the centuries took the simple road of accepting the stories at the beginning of the Bible as historical fact, because it was inspired by God, and they had as yet no sense of modern historical criticism. It is only recently, that modern methods have cast doubt on the early stories in the Bible. And that has led the Church in our day to understand that these tales were inspired by God to teach us the fundamentals about our creation and our fall into sin, and not about the exact history whose details are lost in the mist of time. It is through the meanings hidden within the scriptures that we are enlightened about God and humanity. There we discover not accurate history, but the truths on which we can and must base our certainties about creation, fall and redemption.

Original Innocence

Possibly the most problematic element in these stories for modern people is the teaching that humanity existed in a state of innocence until they sinned by eating the forbidden fruit of knowledge of good and evil. It is hard to imagine such a state when we think in terms of gradual evolution. But it is obvious that there was a point where God breathed into our forebears a soul making them human. What is fundamentally taught in scripture is that soon after this happened, the newly created human beings used their freedom to know evil as well as good, thereby seizing control of creation instead of submitting to God's supremacy which was the true path to happiness. Again we believe that this is a fundamental fact revealed by God. We are not told the historical details of this Fall of mankind into sin, only the veiled account in the third chapter of Genesis. While our own immediate experience is of a world full of evil, it is undeniable that we all harbour a stubborn sense that perfect goodness can exist and that true innocence is possible. This recurring longing for perfection in mankind is not just idle imagination. Genesis 3 clearly teaches that it is our origin, and, in promising that the '*Offspring*' of the '*Woman*'[25] would crush the head of the Serpent, it would once more be our destiny.

In seeking the deep meaning of scripture, we follow Jesus our teacher who used the scriptures in this way – as the source of truth – truth as revealed by our Father God. Christian life is a continual seeking to know to the fullest the God who has revealed himself to us. It is not a body of knowledge that we seek, but to encounter God. Ultimately, that means allowing Christ to form a personal

---

[25] Gen 3: 15

relationship with us. He is God's Word become flesh. He is the complete self-revelation of God.

We also constantly seek to understand our own glorious identity. We *'are a chosen race, a royal priesthood, a consecrated nation, a people set apart to sing the praises of God who called you out of the darkness into his wonderful light.'*[26] This is the identity every baptised person is on the path to discovering. It is the destiny of every human person.

---

[26] 1 Pt 2: 9

Chapter 4

OUR DESTINY

The call to be the Royal Priests of all creation

We are familiar with the statement that every baptised person has been made part of the Royal Priesthood, but it can be difficult to grasp the supreme dignity that has been bestowed upon us. It can be hard to feel that we are Royal or to identify with the description that we are Priests and Priestesses.[27] Yet it was for this that we were made; it is the inheritance that our Lord died to gain for us. It is important to reflect on this great reality.

Scripture tells us that, in the beginning, the Spirit hovered over creation bringing order from chaos, gradually leading to the coming of mankind. It paints the picture of Adam and Eve living in a garden of beauty and life.[28] It is a picture of all creation looking towards God and thrilling with his presence. They were appointed to be the curators of this song of joy and were given the official work of channelling all creation's worship straight to God. They were to turn

---

[27] 'Priestess' is not used in Catholic theology, but given modern gender sensitivity, I have used it here.
[28] Gn 1: 31

every act into a moment of love, praising him for his bounty and drinking deeply of his nurturing kindness. They walked with him in the cool of the evening; they were the King and Queen. In the midst of creation, their joy was to be found in worshiping the Creator in whose image they were made. Their very creation was their ordination as Royal Priests. It was and still is the root of their being – of their humanity and it is also the root of our very being.

It is evident that the process of their creation was not complete; they were on an earthly journey developing under God's guidance into the perfection which would enable them to transit into the full life of heaven. Just as the first book of the Bible tells us about them, the last book, Revelation, gives us an impression of heaven. It is painted in earthly pictures, but the crux is a vision of the mind blowing love affair of the Father and the Son, into which they delight to draw all of creation. The name of the very personal love affair is the Holy Spirit. The response of all redeemed creation is worship.

Our word 'worship' is tainted by our experience of boredom in prayer which even at times is painful. But in heaven there is no boredom or pain, only utterly liberating joy as we dive together into the limitless depths of God's love for us and respond with ever increasing devotion. Maybe a better word than *worship* is *Liturgy*, the Greek for 'the activity of the people'. It is a good word, because it emphasises that worshiping/praising God is the activity we are made for.

After the Fall

Adam and Eve tried to hijack their own development, and in doing so shattered the working of God's wise plan. Basically they and their descendants put themselves in the place of God, and, in their restriction, turned from being royal curators of creation to dominating and forcing creation in attempts to fill the sad emptiness of their own appetites. In subsequent generations, people quickly turned to dominating each other and kingship became confined to those who could seize power and defend it against all claimants. Priesthood too became the domain of a few, who came to represent everyone else in their dealings with God. The lovely appointment of every man and woman as royal priests was gone. It was like providing someone with a deep capacity for love, and them choosing to be in solitary confinement instead. The deepest yearning of the human heart is for God and God was absent. It was not that God had walked away. We had.

Over the centuries, human beings constructed many forms of religion, through which they hoped to fill the emptiness at the centre of their beings. These systems usually arose from charismatic individuals who could rationalise our human emotions to give a temporary sense of connection with the divine - especially impressive if a state of exaltation could be achieved. Furthermore they and their disciples elaborated moral codes within their religious frameworks, which gave some sense of justice and order in a chaotic world.

One essential factor in all religions was the spiritual sense of another reality above and within the material world. People had a belief that somehow there exists a reality that is sacred. But the years have rolled on and increasingly the *'knowledge of good and evil'*[29] that Adam and Eve chose has become more intellectually confined. The stress on rational knowledge is narrowing our outlook and driving out the sense of the sacred. That is leaving mankind fixed in materialism and pragmatic activity, through which we think we can quantify and control our difficult world and somehow find satisfaction. Instead we find a thousand conflicting theories which offer lame explanations of the deeper mysteries of life.

If God had not intervened in our story to turn us round, it would have ended in self-destruction as we flee along ever more perilous paths unleashing dangerous forces which we convince ourselves will empower us and make our plans prosper. But, if we cannot control ourselves, how, ultimately, can we expect to control nature which has had its explosive power released?

The Old Covenant Priesthood

God has intervened. It really began when he forged an alliance with Abraham and his descendants.[30] In his dealings with them over 2000 years, he gradually unveiled himself to them and gradually taught them about their own selves. He began by leading them through the first years of wandering in Canaan, and

---

[29] Gn 3: 6
[30] Gn 17: 12

then of bondage in Egypt. That period ended with their dramatic and miraculous delivery from slavery to Pharaoh, and God brought them to make solemn Covenant with him at Mount Sinai.[31]

In his fearsome apparition to Moses on the mountain top he revealed his plan for them: '*I will count you a kingdom of priests, a consecrated nation.*'[32] His intention was to restore to them all the kingly priesthood which Adam and Eve had jettisoned. They were to be the instruments for restoring a real relationship with God and of harmony to creation. They were, with his help, to join earth to heaven again. They agreed and made a covenant with God, and their leaders ate a communion meal with God in his fearsome presence on the mountain top.[33]

Moses was then summoned to receive the law which God was to give to this great nation.[34] He was in the heart of the fearsome presence for a long time, during which the people, panicked, backpedalled and repudiated the covenant. The tribe of Levi, to which Moses and his brother Aaron belonged, became the instrument of God's dreadful punishment; at God's command they slaughtered 3000 of the leaders of the rebellion. 'Today,' Moses said, '*you have won yourselves investiture as priests of Yahweh.*'[35] The priesthood was withdrawn from all the people and became the prerogative of the

---

[31] Ex 19 ff
[32] Ex 19: 6
[33] Ex 24: 1-11
[34] Ex 24: 12
[35] Ex 32: 29

Levites. God then laid down how this priesthood was to function.

The second half of the book of Exodus is taken up with detailed instruction from God of how the levitically led worship was to be carried out. They were instructed to construct the Ark of the Covenant and the 'Tent of Meeting' where they were to worship him according to his strict instructions. The next book of the Bible is Leviticus which gives more details about worship and the ritual cleanness which was required of the people in order to become holy enough to worship God. In everything, the priesthood of the Levites was central.

The Tent of Meeting was a representation of God's presence, a mobile Sinai. In its Holy of Holies section, hidden by a huge Veil, the Ark of God was situated. There God rested his foot and only the High Priest was allowed into the presence once a year on the Day of Atonement (the day of at-one-ment) when sin was expunged and the Covenant renewed. This became the Temple of Jerusalem. Sinai was now permanent.

As well as the presence of God being focused there, it gradually dawned on them that their worship which God had prescribed, was in fact a making present of the glorious Liturgy of heaven. This was indeed a clouded representation of heaven, but, increasingly, they were promised a new and eternal Covenant and the establishment of an everlasting kingdom for them in the future. They even heard indications that this would extend to all mankind, not just themselves, the

Israelites; that that would be their kingdom and they would all be priests.[36] The Royal Priesthood that Adam and Eve had so wonderfully enjoyed and sadly terminated, was to be restored to all mankind.

Bloody sacrifice

It is very strange to us, that the bloody sacrificing of animals was central to their worship. It seems barbaric, but God dealt with people as he found them and they were barbaric. If kings made treaties together, they symbolised it with the slaughter of an animal through shedding its blood. Blood was for them the life of an animal. It was commonly sprinkled on both treaty makers and symbolised that their agreement was a matter of life and death, and that breaking the agreement was to be punished by death. The treaty (or Covenant) was sealed in blood and ratified by a communion meal in which parts of the victim were often shared. The same model was used even more where people sought to enter into a favourable relationship with their god(s). The more solemn the worship, the greater the size of their sacrifices. When the true God began a personal unveiling of himself to Israel, he used the model they were familiar with: bloody sacrifice.

In the fullness of time, at the final point of God's self-revelation, the Second Person of the Triune God, became flesh in order to establish the New and eternal Covenant. There are vast treasuries of deep meanings in his life, death and resurrection, but the salient point here is that

---

[36] Ex 19: 6

he accomplished the New Covenant by acting both as High Priest and as the victim in the bloody sacrifice of the cross. He replaced the continually repeated Old Covenant worship with the one eternal sacrifice of Calvary. And, whereas the old Temple worship was an annual representation of the Liturgy of heaven, Christ's sacrifice on the cross was the real descent of that Liturgy into the most adverse and horrific of human conditions and completely outweighs any and all that is negative in humanity.

The Old Testament worship was imperfect because the blood of animals was unable to really bring about Atonement. That worship was a gift of God to a primitive people at the beginning of Salvation History thousands of years ago, to enable them to hope for redemption, and to mark out the conditions under which the perfect worship would happen. The High Priests were imperfect sinners like all mankind and approached the Holy of Holies in fear after many ritual cleansings, but ritual did not make them clean inside. Jesus the perfect human being, clean inside and out, replaced once and for all the old Levitical High Priesthood. No animals blood could really seal the Covenant that mankind needed to make with God. But the blood of the perfect unblemished victim, Christ, accomplished it for all eternity. At the moment of his victorious dying into his Father's arms, the old Veil of the Temple was torn from top to bottom. The barrier between us and the Father is now destroyed.

When all was accomplished, blood and water flowed from the pierced heart of Jesus as his body hung on the cross.[37] The water from his side became the tide of Baptism by which he incorporates men and women into his very self and shares with them his relationship to the Father. We receive birth as the sons and daughters of God and we are restored to the Royal Priesthood. And, wonder of wonders, the blood has become the communion meal of the new covenant, the Eucharist in which the sacrifice of the cross is made present in our time and we are drawn up into the liturgy of heaven. In mysterious reality, his body and blood, separated for us in the one eternal sacrifice of the cross, is present and, as we eat and drink, we have communion with the resurrected Son of God. Through this communion, the Church is reinforced as the new Mystical Body of Christ whose physical body has ascended to heaven. His Church is the ingathering of humanity into the Royal Priesthood.

---

[37] Jn 19: 34

Chapter 5

HOW OUR ROYAL PRIESTHOOD WORKS

How does our Royal Priesthood function? First of all, it appoints us to be curators of God's creation like Adam and Eve. We are called to serve the creatures he has placed us among, from the rocks and stones to the plants and animals and the people: everything that makes the world a song of life to God. In our care and nurturing, our protecting and developing we seek to love as God loves all he has made, and we seek to bring it to the best we can help it to be, as an act of love to the Father. That is the true meaning of sacrifice.

Next, we have to understand that we are not the chief curators of the corner of creation where he has placed us - he is. We are his assistants. We study him and learn from him, and he inspires us not just intellectually and emotionally, but breathes his Holy Spirit deep into our spirit, into those mysterious regions of our being where we are being moulded by his loving hands. Familiarity with Jesus is primary; from that relationship all our collaboration with God proceeds.

Realism and development

All this may sound poetic and maybe a bit idealistic, but it is entirely practical. Much of the world we live in is damaged and impaired and needs repairing. That can require us to work long hours often in discomfort and monotony, but, if we forget that we are working alongside and for Christ, we lose ourselves in the activity and disconnect ourselves from the loving creator who alone illuminates all we do with meaning. With Christ, we can turn everything into an act of love for the Father, and only in that context, can we fully love and enjoy his creatures, and truly fall in love with our brother and sister human beings. Like the world we live in, we are each of us evolving and we need patience as God develops us into his *'works of art'*.[38] Our priesthood that we were appointed to at baptism develops gradually as we learn wisdom under the caring hand of God.

As priests, each of us is commissioned to bring every part of our lives as an offering of love to God, and in so far as we assist things to be ordered according to God's design, we are sharing the royal role. All of us are called to be royal priests. It is distorting and false to continue thinking of priesthood as a lone individual mediating with God on behalf of many others, or, more tellingly, one who exercises power over a religious grouping. There is only one priest now, Christ, and he delights in sharing that role with all who will walk with him.

---

[38] Eph 2: 110

Loving service

In his kingship, he has declined to exercise any other power than truth, justice and love. We see this supremely at work in his utter abandonment of power as he is being crucified. He only loves: he forgives his executioners, thirsts for people to be born into his new creation, gives his extraordinary mother to nurture the world, assures a criminal of paradise that day, and calls into the heart of the centurion overseeing his execution.

Where he has come from and is returning to is the Father, the heart of utter devotion burning in the life of the Trinity. He came to unveil the Trinity, the last stage of God's unveiling. In the family of the Trinity utter devotion is expressed in the loving gift of oneself to the other and the blissful receiving of the other. God's love is urgent to be expressed in us here on earth as loving service and can only flourish through our receiving his dear love. He proclaims that the greatest human being is the one who most serves all,[39] and states that what will convince the world that he has truly come among us is the Trinitarian love which binds his followers together.[40]

We have to lose the notion that kingship is about any other form of power. The royal priest/priestess only claims the power to cherish and be cherished and to serve all in that spirit. It is true that earthly kings and queens need to have peacekeeping forces to protect against violence and curtail real and present evil, but

---

[39] Jn 19: 34, Mt 23: 11; Mk 9: 35
[40] Jn 18: 22-23

that should be for the service of the common good not power for its own sake. Also anger like that which empowered Jesus to cleanse the temple of its market stalls[41] is necessary in some situations, but temper is only valid when it is tempered by love. Truly great kings and queens give themselves in service to their people, forgetting themselves so that all may flourish peacefully to the greatest extent. As we exercise our priesthood of care and service we partake in the Kingly function of Christ, the restorer of creation.

Spiritual sacrifice involves the Cross

This is no rose-tinted vocation that we have. The way to resurrection is through the cross, which he warns us must be picked up each day by his followers. To be agents of Christ's love requires that we acknowledge that we will suffer in order to bring the liberation of the children of God to our frustrated creation.[42]

The New Testament changes the ordinary word for love or affection to a new Greek word, *Agape*, which St Paul states is *'the highest gift (of God)'*.[43] It is not equivalent to our normal human loving, but must be requested and freely given. It supercharges human loving with God's own love. With this empowerment from Christ we can scale mountains and endure everything. And it is crucial to accept that this empowerment is not only for great challenges, but

---

[41] Mk 11:15-1; Lk 19; 45-47; Jn 2:14-16
[42] Rom 8: 22
[43] 1 Cor 13

especially for ordinary little services which often need to be repeated for years. It is through each little step, through each prayer, each tear, each act of service, as long as we are harnessed to Christ, that the royal priests haul creation into the glorious liberation of the children of God. Creation is so full of hope! It longs for *'the glorious liberation of the children of God'*.[44]

The interior kingdom

This chapter's emphasis has been on how we function as royal priests externally; that is the actions we carry out to order creation as one great act of love to the Father. But it is important to emphasise that for all such action to have maximum effect it must spring from the interior prayer activity of our heart. There we increasingly move as partakers in the very life of God the Son. For Jesus, all his actions flowed out of his ardent love for his Father. Loving the Father and being loved by the Father is the very essence of Jesus' being. We who share his life, who live in him and have him living in us, are first of all worshipers. From this deep prayer within, flow all our deeds as kingly priests.

As well as the Kingdom of God coming "on earth as it is in heaven" for which we are privileged to labour, there is in each of us an interior kingdom where we grow in love and identity with Christ living within us, and which leads us gradually to perceive all the world through the eyes of the royal compassion and mercy of God. All too often the interior life of worship is

---

[44] Rom 8: 22

neglected with the effect that our royal priesthood is nebulous and stuttering. Or we become just another political movement with a "Catholic" label.

Confident intercession

Jesus spends much of his time calling people to ask in faith. There is something in the children of God's expectant requests that releases floods of grace. More than direct action or purposeful programmes, intercession gets results. But there is something distinctive we need to remember about the intercession of Christ's royal priests; it is full of confidence in our Father.

We naturally sympathise and empathise with tragedy and suffering when we encounter it, and the pain and the woe can overcome us. Christ wept for hard-hearted Jerusalem,[45] and cried at the waste of the life of Lazarus[46] and the distress of his sisters. But he did not become fixated with the negatives, he raised his eyes to his Father[47] and re-immersed himself in the Father's all-embracing, totally determined plan for our good salvation, and the Father's infinite power to bless and heal. It was in that utter conviction that he called down blessings on the tragic plights people brought to him, and he always transformed them.

His blessings are not all immediately obvious; he knew that his Father's intervention is often deeper than first became apparent. He healed hundreds, but hid

---

[45] Lk 19: 41
[46] Jn 11: 35
[47] Jn 11:41

himself when people only wanted physical healing.[48] The nine healed lepers[49] caused him profound grief because they, unlike the Samaritan,[50] had not been aware of the deeper healing of their spirits that he was offering. They would be sick again, but their spirits, once ignited with the divine fire, would only have grown. As royal priests, we are to bless in the same way, with confidence not focusing on the tragic, but confidently calling God's constant grace into the situation we are praying about. In this way we bless. It is an integral part of the royal priesthood that royal priests bless.

Most of us are not accustomed to doing this openly; it is well worth doing. You would be amazed at the response when you say 'God bless' to someone who has delivered you a parcel or to the clerk at the supermarket checkout. They often pause for a moment. On one occasion on ending a conversation with a computer technician in India, I said 'Thankyou and God bless'. His response was 'no one had ever said that to me before. Thankyou'.

The Ministerial Priesthood is different from the Royal Priesthood of all the baptised

Today, we normally use the word *priest* to mean 'the person chosen by the Church to lead a Church community'; that is the Ministerial Priesthood of

---

[48] Cf Mk 1: 45
[49] Lk 17: 17
[50] Lk 17: 19

Bishops, Priests[51] and Deacons. There is much debate today about that priesthood. Some of our Protestant friends deny that it exists, even in the face of the evident instituting of the episcopate, presbyterate and the diaconate by the apostles. When carried out in a spirit of service it is a beautiful, enriching gift of God.

Christ gifts individuals with special charisms for works of service in the Church. Ephesians[52] describes the main ones:

> *'And to some his gift was that they should be apostles; to some, prophets; to some, evangelists; to some, pastors and teachers; so that the saints together make a unity in the work of service, building up the body of Christ.'*

St Paul says in 1 Timothy:[53] *'The saying is trustworthy: If anyone aspires to the office of presiding elder (presbyter), he desires a noble task'* and then Paul proceeds to give criteria for their appointment. Later he does the same for deacons. The letter to the Hebrews[54] says: *'Obey your leaders and submit to them, for they are keeping watch over your souls'*. The offices of bishop, presbyter and deacon are gifts of God to the Church. They do not replace the Royal Priesthood of all the baptised, but only function well when they serve it. Their service is to nourish the order and communion

---

[51] Normally called "Presbyters" or "Presiding Elders" in the New Testament
[52] Eph 4: 11-13
[53] 1 Tm 3: 1-7
[54] Heb 13: 17

needed for the Church to flourish, and, under the Spirit, to guide it. They bring the gift of order to the Church. Their role is a sacrament, an outward sign of God's grace to confirm the brotherhood.

The Sacrament of Orders, is not about giving orders. It is the special grace by which God maintains the oneness and order in his Church. The Spirit pours out his graces on each baptised person. Each of us is called to exercise our Royal Priesthood in a unique way, but no one can grasp the fullness of God's rich outpouring of all the different roles to all the individuals in the growing of the Kingdom. It is through the Sacrament of Orders, that God guarantees that, gently but surely, the many rich vocations and charisms do not descend into chaos but are held together in a bond of brotherly love. You have only to read the letters of St Paul to the Corinthians to see this Sacrament in operation.

When Hebrews exhorts us to '*obey your leaders*', it is not with the blind obedience which many of the lords of this world require. The latin word *obaudire* means 'to stop and listen deeply'. It requires us to exercise our discernment under the guidance of the Holy Spirit and to do so respecting the role of the one who speaks. The Spirit speaks through all the members of the Church, and listening needs to be exercised both ways as Pope Francis teaches, but it is the Pope and the bishops who have final responsibility for discerning the guidance of the Spirit.

You might expect that this Ministerial Priesthood would be defined by regulations and protocols about leadership and entitlement, but in fact it begins with 'prayer and the service of the word'.[55] It arises from making the Eucharist present, which is the source of Church community and life, together with ensuring that the people are nourished by the teaching of the Apostles and the Scriptures.

During the second phase of the Church, Bishops and Priests very often exercised strong leadership which relied on the laity following willingly. Perhaps some of this was because so many Christians only had a weak grasp of the faith and firm authority was necessary. In the third phase of the Church the roles of Bishops and Priests and Deacons will evolve as more and more lay people are led into greater maturity by the Spirit.

The Royal Priesthood calls all of us to greater maturity - a new heart and a new mind[56]

In this third phase of the Church, the Spirit is urgent to lead us and the world more profoundly into the new humanity. The letter to the Ephesians which was written to stir up and refresh the faith of the second generation of Christians says: *'Your mind must be renewed by a spiritual revolution so that you can put on the new self that has been created in God's way, in the goodness and holiness of the truth'.*[57] Today we are being led into nothing less than a refreshing of this spiritual revolution.

---

[55] Acts 6: 4
[56] Ez 36: 26
[57] Eph 4: 23-24

In his letter to the Romans, St Paul urges us *to 'think of God's mercy, my brothers, and worship him, I beg you, in a way that is worthy of thinking beings'.*[58] Here again is the call for a *'renewed mind'.*[59] It will be necessary for us Catholics, as we own more strongly our royal priesthood, to think more deeply, to become more familiar with the story of salvation through scripture and to have a better sense of how salvation has progressed through the lives of holy people over the last two thousand years, and also to grasp afresh the wonders of Church teaching. This *renewed mind* is what it means to be proactive. Rather than react to what the world hollers at us, we must turn more strongly to what God is saying.

As this process gathers strength in the third phase which is now beginning, each of us will appreciate more profoundly our call to take our part in the Royal Priesthood offering our *'living bodies as a holy sacrifice, truly pleasing to God',* not modelling ourselves *'on the behaviour of the world around'* us, but letting our *'behaviour change, modelled by our new mind'.*[60]

'Father, may they be one in us that the world may believe that you have sent me'[61]

Both Ephesians and Romans go on to stress that we must listen in love to what the Spirit is saying through

---

[58] Rom 12: 1
[59] Eph 4: 23
[60] Rom 12: 2
[61] Jn 17: 21

each other. Too often in the past, the spirit of division and contention has impeded the work of the Holy Spirit. The path opening before us now calls for great love, great listening and deep prayer for the gift of discerning what the Holy Spirit is saying to the Church.

The greatest danger as we enter this third stage is pride, which exaggerates our own opinions and views, as opposed to humility which patiently seeks unity through truth. In the story of the Tower of Babel we are told that God struck the proud builders of their own tower to heaven by confusing their language. I believe that the true meaning of the story is that people could not understand each other, because that they stopped listening to God and to each other. When the Holy Spirit came upon the Church at Pentecost, he signalled his presence by enabling people of many languages to hear the same message as they opened their spirits to listen to his voice. That moment of wondrous unity was his demonstration of what he has come to bring: unity and peace, but it will only come as, together, we open completely to his inspiration.

Later in this book, I will attempt to give some reflections on this process of openness to the Spirit. But, in the next three chapters, I want to expand on some of the elements we need to focus on in order to receive a *renewal of our minds*. We need as Catholics to renew our grasp of the basics of God's teaching in three areas: Scripture, the story of the Church, and the teachings of the Church.

Chapter 6

KNOWING THE SCRIPTURES

Catholics and the Scriptures

Our faith is based on the Sacred Scriptures. We Catholics normally learn the scriptures in the context of hearing them at Mass on Sunday. This can cause us to develop an uncoordinated and partial grasp of it. It is very important to develop a whole view as well.

Take the reading from 1 Corinthians 7:29-31 which is the second reading on the Third Sunday of the Year in cycle B:

'Brothers: our time is growing short. Those who have wives should live as though they had none, and those who mourn should live as though they had nothing to mourn for; those who are enjoying life should live as though there were nothing to laugh about; those whose life is buying things should live as though they had nothing of their own; and those who have to deal with the world should not become engrossed in it. I say this because the world as we know it is passing away.'

Read out baldly on a Sunday, this text can give the impression that St Paul is anti-marriage, anti-fun and anti-trade. It seems tantamount to his advising us to be miserable. But if you look at the whole of Chapter 7 in 1 Corinthians you see a much more balanced picture.

The Chapter begins with an explanation that he is answering various questions that have been put to him in a letter from the Church in Corinth. These cover many aspects of Christian life but the first questions answered are about marriage, sexuality and virginity. In the first part he advises that it is better to marry than be tortured by sexual desire. Then he goes on to state that the only thing he has clearly from the Lord in answer to their queries is that married people should stay together. Then he goes on to state explicitly that the rest of his advice is from himself. He concludes the chapter by repeating that these thoughts are from himself, and says that he offers them believing that he has the Spirit guiding him. This is very cautious of St Paul; he usually is far more directive. But when you consider that the beginning and end of the text shows that he assumes the end of the world is very near, then it is obvious that what he thinks was inspired by the Holy Spirit can only a be partially inspired since the world did not end.

The vast majority of the chapter repeatedly shows that he supports marriage, as well as supporting celibacy for the sake of the Kingdom. When Paul stresses that some of the things he writes are his own opinions, he is encouraging us to listen and make up our own minds. But in doing so in our day and age, we should seek to be guided by the same

Spirit as Paul sought to be guided by. What I personally take from this chapter and other New Testament readings is:

1. Marriage is God's gift to Adam and Eve and all their descendants.
2. We are not to base our lives on the expectation that the world is going to end imminently. It will one day, possibly sooner than we think, but any consideration that the end may come imminently cannot negate the probability that we have a long time to wait. Therefore engagement in the world's affairs is imperative. Are we not the custodians of creation and responsible for justice and peace among human beings?
3. Eventually the things of this world will pass away, when Christ returns and a whole new and eternal order of the universe will begin. With that in mind, we must see the things of earth as temporary, even marriage and commerce and we have to conduct ourselves in love of God and service of others. We are already members of the new creation by living in the Holy Spirit. So we should not act in sexual or business ways like the rest of the world, but be responsible to God not the forces of human desire or the so called, laws of commerce like 'business is business'. And we are called to persuade others to act in the same way – love, peace, justice and happiness will only flourish following the guidance of God.
4. Celibacy for the sake of the kingdom is as real a vocation today as in the time of Paul. He saw clearly that God would always call men and women

to be *'Eunuchs for the sake of the kingdom'*.[62] This does not make them better people, but equal to the married in service of the Kingdom.

Scripture should always be read in its context in order to really hear the word of God. It is always meant to be an encounter with Christ, the real Word of God. The more we take the time and effort to ponder it and plumb its depths, the more Jesus reveals himself to us and shows us the way to the Father.

Christ's followers encounter him in the Scriptures

If we compare Christian understanding of the Bible with the Muslim Koran, we see a stark difference. Muslims see the Koran as a direct revelation of God dictated to Mohammed. It is in Arabic, and it is the absolute message of God; not a word can be changed, neither should it be translated into another language. To read it one must learn Arabic. For us Christians, the Bible is a collection of books which have been selected by the Jewish authorities and the Church as definitely inspired by God in his process of revealing himself to humanity. What is inspired is not every word and detail, but we have to read the Bible intelligently and prayerfully to find the sense of what God is revealing to us about himself and about ourselves.

It is his **word**. We read it not in a rigid way, but as a living word, alive and active as we read it. Through it,

---

[62] Mt 19: 12

the Word made flesh wishes to speak to us here and now. It is dynamic. The more we study it prayerfully, the more Christ speaks to us words that make our hearts burn. It is a great loss to treat it only as a formal part of the Church's ritual to be heard at Mass in a mysterious way. It demands understanding and study. This need not be academic, but informed enough to know the context of what we are reading or hearing, and it is especially inspiring when done with others.

Incidentally, St Paul repeats again and again that, far from causing us to be miserable, living with and in Jesus gives us joy that far outweighs the joys that this world offers.

Chapter 7

THE REASON FOR OUR HOPE

God's wonderful light

St Peter teaches: *'You are royal priests, a holy nation, God's very own possession, a people set apart to sing the praises of God who called you out of the darkness into his wonderful light'*.[63] We Catholics have no difficulty in accepting St Peter's description of our wonderful identity.

But, when he goes on to say: *'Always be prepared to give an answer to everyone who asks you to give the reason for the hope that you have'*,[64] we find that bit difficult. I have known many saintly, self-sacrificing Catholic people who shine the light in various ways, but most declare that they do not know how to speak in answer to St Peter's call to give an answer to those who ask the reason for our hope. Somehow our catechesis[65] has helped people to shine the *'wonderful light'* but not enabled our people, who have *'gentleness and respect'* in plenty, to *'give the answers'* for their hope.

---

[63] 1 Pt 2: 9
[64] 1 Pt 3: 15
[65] Catechesis is the teaching of the faith - Directory of Catechesis, Catholic Truth Society [2020] para 55-56

For example many Mass going Catholics say 'I never talk to my grown up children about the faith, as I don't know what to say to them or how to answer their questions.' And these are people who have been exemplary parents, and outstanding in their careers, mastering the skills and knowledge this required.

The beautiful Ocean

Have we taught people through concepts and words about the beautiful ocean of the 'goodness of God', and not helped them stand on the shore in wonder or encouraged them to surf freely and dive into the freshness of its truth? The Deposit of Faith, the teachings guarded and laboured over by the Church for centuries, is not a mere text book to be learnt, but the gift of God's revelation of himself as recorded in scripture and experienced by saintly men and women for 2000 years. Its richness should excite us and cause us to bring others to meet that God who is urgent to reveal himself. It is the Good News (Gospel) that Jesus spoke of.

Some time ago, we put on a two-year course in the parish in collaboration with the School of the Annunciation operating at that time out of Buckfast Abbey. Over 20 people joined. All said as they went along: 'why did no one tell us all this before?' They felt that they were moving from a more or less notional grasp of the faith to a personal process of discovering the riches of revelation. It left all of them wanting more.

Using the Catechism of the Catholic Church, the course sought to acquaint the parishioners with the foundations of the faith in a fresh and dynamic way. It involved prayer, reading and personal teaching with a one-to-one element as well as group discussion. People soon began to develop at their own pace, and we began to understand a lot about how adults learn. Some needed more discussion, some needed study through reading. Some only had time for a light approach, others wanted to go into more depth. There is a whole exceedingly fruitful and essential field here to be developed in our parishes. Anne Bardell expounds this more fully in the final section of this book.

The course placed as its aim helping people become engaged in the New Evangelisation. What was wonderful was that about twelve of them joined a parish Evangelisation Group at the end of the course. Before we left the parish the Evangelisation Group, together with ourselves, put on, for two successive years, a six-part programme called *Discovering Christ*[66] for the parents of first communion children and other interested parishioners. It was like an Alpha Course but shorter. Each evening there was a meal and presentations and discussion. It culminated in a day retreat. It was wonderful to see how the leaders grew in confidence and skills. The parents all said they had come closer to Christ and to the Church, and quite a few became Mass attenders, while others appreciated being recognised as important to the Church which they had not previously felt. All the parents were empowered to accompany their children in the

---

[66] A seven-week course from the Christ Life Catholic Ministry for Evangelisation of Canada (Christlife.org)

Communion preparation. We saw this programme as training the Parents who are *'the primary and most important educators of their children'*[67] to be their first catechists. The parishioners who were not parents of the Sacramental Programme were similarly enthused.

The study of God is theology. For teachers in the Church, it is a lifelong science. But for the rest of us, it is the way to prepare for prayer, our conversation with the Father through and with Jesus. Each of us needs a basic grasp of the fundamentals of our faith, suitable to our minds and lifestyles, but it needs to come to us as revelation, filled with wonder, whetting our appetite for more. It must lead firstly to prayer and secondly to mental retention. When Catholics learn about their faith as a subject in school or Church without discovering God personally through it, they will not have grasped the real depth of the faith and it will not stay; and they will drift away.

In our various attempts to help parishioners gain a basic grasp of the fundamentals of our faith we have realised that everyone is different, and there are many ways of grasping the different elements and treasures of Church teaching. We firmly believe that guides are needed who can lead individuals and groups to access the learning materials that best suit them. Today there is some wonderful material available, although it is important to check that the material is Catholic. We need to empower guides to discern what is suitable for

---

[67] St Pope John Paul II, (23 May 2004) *38th World Communications Day Message* [online]. Rome. Holy See No. 5

the people they are helping, and to know what is available. The aim is to help Catholics have a coherent grasp of the basics, which is inspiring and sufficient to give them confidence to begin answering the enquiries of people who come searching.

We have found that working in groups, coupled to private exploration of the faith, is very effective. The Holy Spirit speaks through fellow group members as well as the guides.

Up to the present time, most of the Church's effort in adult learning has gone into providing academic training for leaders in faith formation. There is very little provision of what most Catholics need, namely shorter more intimate courses that feed their thirst for knowledge of God. We have seen how people drink in the new found knowledge as though they will never find such an oasis again in their lives. For a long time there has been talk of Catholic Adult Faith Formation. It is time the Church put much more effort into this. *The Acts of the Apostles* describes the first Church in Jerusalem in this way: *'These remained faithful to the teaching of the apostles, to the brotherhood, to the breaking of bread and to the prayers'.*[68] Helping people to be *'faithful to the teaching of the Apostles'* is urgently needed today.

The second chapter of this book underlined the crucial need to know Jesus personally. Every Catholic who enjoys this relationship can surely begin

---

[68] Acts 2: 42

to explain even simply and timidly how he is the reason for their hope. He has promised that his Spirit would empower them to do so, but a growing awareness of the richness of Church teaching will embolden and strengthen their witness.

Chapter 8

AWARE OF THE CHURCH'S STORY

Reformation

During the middle ages, the Church had drifted into bad habits, and a renewal was needed. Latin remained the language of public worship long after most people stopped understanding it, which resulted in the richness of Scripture being locked away from the people. The emerging clerical cast made religion their speciality leaving many people ignorant of the riches of the faith; in fact, many of the clergy themselves were badly trained as well. Without good teaching people will construct their own blend of piety, and folk-lore will take the place of the knowledge of God.

The Reformation movement was a huge reaction to these shortcomings. It largely sprang from the rediscovery of the Scriptures as they were translated into modern languages, and the new printing presses made them widely available. Scripture tells the story of how God relates to human beings, and the reformers stressed the need for a deeper sense of personal relationship with God. They claimed that the Catholicism of their day was failing in a large part to bring people to this and they increasingly protested at this failure. The movement became known as the Protestant Reformation. Many of their points were right; some wrong as they struggled with the question of how justification in the sight of God came about. Things gradually deteriorated into quarrels, and then violent conflict.

Healing and wholeness

The following centuries of disunity gravely wounded the Church; people forgot that the first sign of Christ's presence is the love his disciples have for one another. Dispute replaced the Spirit's gift of solidarity which is God's way of ensuring the gradual and peaceful development of Christianity and of Christianity's effect on the world.

Really, both sides of the argument had valid points to make, but the Reformers became too fixed on the faults they diagnosed and laboured over them. In the Catholic Counter Reformation, the Church reacted to the mistakes of the protestant reformers and narrowed its own teaching very much to refute them. The Church of Jesus was wounded and impaired. Disagreements can be a positive force in dialogue, but, in conflict, they restrict the participants and narrow the search for truth. The children of God, who are supposed to be the light of the world instead become the same as the world. A renewed opening to the Holy Spirit was needed.

Such an opening is impossible unless Christians realise their poverty of spirit and turn to the Lord for his help. This poverty is being gifted to us in our day as we see many people ceasing to find Christianity relevant.

We have been led to a renewed and humbler search for what the Spirit is saying to the Churches, which, among other things, must lead to an increasing study of the depths and riches which God has inspired throughout the first two thousand years of Christianity. In discovering what was best in the lives of our brother and sisters who have walked with Christ in the Church before us, and recognising their errors, we will be led to a renewed revival of the One Holy Catholic and Apostolic Faith.

A simple account of our story

My thumbnail sketch above attempting to discern currents present in the Church throughout the past few centuries can be contradicted in many ways. It is simplistic, but, I hope, helpful. It is important to make sense of how we have come to our moment in time in order to be able to move forward. It is a pastor's reflection on fifty years of experience of what has been happening in the vineyard of Christ. In a similar way, most Catholics would benefit from gaining a simple foundation in the history of the Church.

One huge factor which is overlooked in the thoughts I have offered is the evident continual holiness and graced lives of countless people throughout the time I focus on. God has not deserted his Church, but he does want to shine through it more effectively.

Engaging with the process

I think that what I am trying to say is that we should help people engage with the process of what the Holy

Spirit is gradually doing in the Church. So often one or two instances in our own experience form the basis of how each of us sees the Church. We adopt formulas like: 'it is too clerical; it is out of date; it is all about liberation; people never learn; we need women priests, et cetera' and we get stuck. We are so prone to focus on solutions to issues which are frustratingly obvious to ourselves that we fail to see the ark of history. That is the big picture of what God is doing and therefore how we fit into it.

Let me give an example of the process which has been going on in my life time: the Second Vatican Council. Many people ask what has happened to it, by which they mean: has it had any effect apart from the Mass being in English? Others ask: why are the bits of its teaching that have made sense to me not been fully implemented? It happened fifty years ago, why are things so slow?

If we ask what the Vatican Council really taught, we find that the principle themes were: the laity – their dignity and call into the shared Royal Priesthood of all the baptised; the need for the treasures of Scripture to be opened up; the renewed vision of the Church as God's leaven in the dough of the world instead of an inward looking society that saw itself perfect and separate; ecumenism; dialogue with other faiths; the need for our liturgy to be reformed; and more. These themes were introduced all together into the reality and practice of the millions and millions of people who form the Church. There followed thousands and thousands of attempts to put into practice what they meant. Some have been foolish, some brilliant, but overall there has been massive movement of the whole Church along the paths of these themes. And it is far from finished; only in the past couple of years has the reality of synodality as applying to all members of the Church come into prominence. Much of the Council focused on the role of Bishops leading to a call for regular Synods of Bishops. In our day, the practice of these Synods has been merged with the other focus of the Council, the increased participation of the laity.

This gradual process of change set in motion by Vatican II is seeping into the lives of all Catholics more and more, truly guided by the Holy Spirit. Considering the number and diversity of all the people involved; there is a remarkable, if sometimes painful, transition taking place. It is hard for each of us to see the great forest of change because we are situated among just a few of its trees, but it is important to grasp that the process is in motion and that it is being led by the Spirit of God. Some of the process seems slow; it is evidently shot through with human mistakes needing corrections; there are tensions of interpretation, but the whole community on countless levels is engaged in producing the fruits of Vatican II.

A simple outline of how change has happened over time in previous epochs of the Church helps people to perceive the ark of God's steady activity as he gradually matures his Church. A simple summary of some of the recent wonderful developments in different parts of the world would encourage us when we feel that progress is slow in our situation, for example the life and work of St Teresa of Calcutta.

Vatican II spotlighted the Church itself

The greatest teaching of Vatican II was about the Church itself. The Council issued four principle documents outlining the fruit of their deliberations called *Constitutions*. Half of these were about the Church. This emphasis on the Church itself was urgently needed. Most of us had notions of what Church is which seriously needed broadening by a fresh look at the Church's roots.

I remember Cardinal Joseph Seunens, one of the chairmen of Vatican II, saying to a group of people: 'Love the Church. Love the Church!' For decades afterwards I wanted to preach about the Church and always felt I couldn't. I could deliver a teaching giving a dry overview of what I had been taught about the Church, but I lacked the dynamism of the love that Seunens spoke about. I had it in my head, and I was committed, but I was not inspired by a vision of Church which touched my heart.

Only recently have I begun to form a vison of this great, lovely, gushing flood of the Spirit of God in our world which we call Church. It lifts millions of people into its flow at the same time. It sparks mysteriously from one to another, it binds very different folk into community. It is never still, ever moving with divine invincibility into new forms and expressions, generation after generation. It is truly the Body of Christ continually awakening and active.

It is you and me, and also countless brothers and sisters who are as yet unaware of how they are involved, but are already producing fruits of the Spirit. It is in reality the core dynamic of humanity, visible and invisible. All humanity stands in relation to the incarnate Son of God and receives inspiration from his Spirit. Those who are unaware of this are like the huge hidden submerged mass of an iceberg. What is commonly described as Church is like the part of the berg that is visible.

The Church is very often spoken of as the hierarchy with all their actions and dramas, but that is a poor simplification of the Spirit's vast, quiet yet inspired activity in countless private souls. In fact the leadership of the Apostles and their successors, the hierarchy, has always had the uncomfortable job of catch-up following the flow of the Holy Spirit and somehow managing to help us all stay together in real communion, and discern the Spirit's lead. They do this through the power of grace, but the operation of grace can be an uncomfortable experience which should not surprise us. We are made in the image of God and not meant for comfortable harbours. True pastors must expect to come at last in front of our Father bloodied and battered like his Beloved Son, and hope to be able to claim that they have played their part with the ability and grace that has been given them. That is enough, and the future is assured.

An overview of Church history prepares us for the future

It is not beyond our power to provide Catholics with a basic account of the history of the Church which would facilitate a greater grasp of how the Holy Spirit works in sinful mankind to gradually bring about redemption. Up until now, most of us have had to be satisfied with anecdotes and being limited to a few highlighted episodes from the Church's story. The abundant riches of God's grace acting within vast human weakness is a story to thrill the soul. It is this faithful activity of God which needs to be witnessed, not dry accounts of events. It is the *story* in *history* which needs to be passed on.

The Old Testament is not a jumbled collection of Jewish thoughts and stories, but is only understood when we read in it the story of God's relationship with Israel, and his continual effort to be with them revealing his love. In the same way, the story of the Church from Pentecost to today is the story of his relationship with all of us. It is our story. Each one of us is in it. If we have a better sense of our past, we will be better enabled to write our chapter in the continuing story of God's Church.

Chapter 9

THE HEART OF CHRISTIANITY

The *'spiritual revolution'*[69] which is Christianity, is deepening and growing into its third phase. In the previous three chapters, I have focused on some of the ways in which we need to prepare for this by a *'renewal of our minds'*.[70] Jesus is preparing his Church to baptise the modern age which is developing through vast, often bewildering, progress in human understanding. Human progress will not fulfil the desire of the human heart for peace and happiness unless it is baptised in the fire of the Holy Spirit. God earnestly desires this. We are at the beginning of a new stage in God's *'plentiful harvest'*.[71]

This epoch of great change that we are living through has such great potential. God is gifting us in the modern age with increasingly deeper insight into our humanity, such as psychology, clearer understanding of human development and vaster knowledge of the world we live in. This is causing a great deal of rethinking; our assumptions about other people and ourselves are being adjusted. The modern age seems at present to be a

---

[69] Cf Eph 4:23-24
[70] ibid
[71] Mt 9:35-38

melting pot of ideas and theories, and these need Christian synthesising. Through the Second Vatican Council, the Spirit called us to take the modern world seriously, to dialogue with it, and to return to the basics of our own revelation and practice in order to effectively bless and enlighten the people of our day. In consequence a renewal of Christianity is developing which is still rather mixed up in most of our minds. The need to purify our thinking under the guidance of the Spirit is urgent. Where do the basics of Christianity lie?

They are fundamentally summed up in John 3:16:

*'**God loved the world so much** that he gave his only Son so that everyone who believes in him may not be lost but may have eternal life. For God sent his Son into the world, not to condemn the world but so that through him the world might be saved'.*

It is the love of God which is the key to everything. That is Christianity's basis.

What does love mean?

The word *'love'* has so many meanings. We naturally think of it in human terms, but the supreme insight of Christianity is that we base our understanding of love on God's love which is very distinct from human loving. To express this the New Testament coins the word *'Agape'*. Human love at its best can be heroic and sometimes seem superhuman. It can not happen without God's help. But it is not always Agape.

We need to understand what Agape is. In the English speaking world many of our bible translations translate Agape as 'Charity'. This word has lost its power since 'Charity' nowadays largely means outreaches to help those in need. Consequently the meaning of Agape has become obscured for many of us.

The word 'Agape' occurs over 200 times in the New Testament. Perhaps the most familiar passage where it is used is in 1 Corinthians 12-13 beginning with:

> 'Be ambitious for the higher gifts, and I am going to show you a way that is better than any of them. If I have all the eloquence of men or of angels but speak without love…'[72]

What is Paul getting at? He is addressing the Church in Corinth which had great spiritual gifts such as prophecy, healing, and words of wisdom, but it was riddled with division. Is he calling the community to have more consideration of each other, even the self-denial which puts others before self? No, he is talking about something much greater, something which heals the heart of the community, which is Agape.

This passage (1 Corinthians 12-13) is used often at Christian weddings, with the intention of expressing the aspirations of those who wish to love wholeheartedly. Implicit in that is a prayer for God to empower us when we find love difficult. That is a gift greatly to be prayed for, and what better way for a couple to plight their troth

---

[72] 1 Cor 12: 31 etc.

than before the Father who alone can empower such love? But few couples imagine what they are truly asking for. Agape is something superior to human love as that is commonly understood.

Paul, uses the Agape word for love in 2 Corinthians 5: 14 when he says *'the love of Christ impels us'*. Translators of the Bible take different stabs at delivering the meaning. Some say it "constrains us", as though we are tied up by it and coerced. Some say "overwhelms us" as though we are lifted to a different dynamic than love as we normally experience it. Some say it "urges" us as though it is a deeply felt need. Clearly, Paul is attempting to describe a different reality to what we normally mean by love, even at its most heroic.

> The Encyclopaedia Britannica defines Agape well:
> **Agape**, *Greek agapē, in the New Testament, **the fatherly love of God for humans**, as well as the **human reciprocal love for God**. In Scripture, the transcendent agape love is the highest form of love and is contrasted with eros, or erotic love, and philia, or brotherly love.*

This rightly states that Agape is the highest form of love, God's love for us and our loving God back. Paul calls it the gift that is *'better than any'*,[73] for which we should *'be ambitious'*.[74] It enters the human heart and transforms it gradually. It is the true meaning of being justified or righteous. By it, our hearts are righted, set

---

[73] Ibid
[74] Ibid

right, stood on their true basis, which is to be the beloved of God. Agape does not spring from our natural human powers to love as we know them. It is the transforming of the heart after it has entered *'the gates of holiness...the Lord's own gate where the just may enter'*.[75] This is a gate which the Lord alone can *'open'*.[76] With it, the human heart is righted, because it was originally and fundamentally made for this divine love to be its primary source of life. We are the beloved children of God beautifully created to live in God's family. That fundamental rightness was gravely upset at the Fall of mankind. But it has been wonderfully restored by Christ's work on Calvary.

Agape is the *'greatest of all'*[77] of the gifts of God, to be sought before all others, because it makes all other loves Christian. It purifies our human love gradually, and must be continually prayed for. In so far as we fall in love with God, we will be enabled to fall in love with everyone.

Contemplation

In the 'Our Father', when Jesus shows us many forms of prayer. He puts first *hallowing the name of the Father*. This is not just praise with lips and songs, but reverence and awe - ultimately adoration. I have seen a group of youngsters joyfully praising God with the

---

[75] Grail Psalm 118: 19-20
[76] Grail Psalm 118: 19
[77] 1 Cor 12: 31

enthusiasm so characteristic of youth, but then become quiet in profound adoration.

The habit of adoration arises from the practice of contemplation. It is distinct from meditation. Meditation is the raising of our minds to God through considering some truth about him which arises from study or spiritual reading or lectio divina or other forms such as the prayer of imagination. It leads to gradual enlightenment, but it usually is an exercise of the intellect which, at its best, can lead our hearts to burn within us. It strengthens conviction and it motivates us to hope. It disposes us to receive the gifts of the Holy Spirit especially wisdom, understanding, and knowledge. It is an essential prayer for maturing Christians, and prompts us to love God. We prepare our minds for it through focusing on truth, and we will often have to keep refocusing because our busy minds are easily distracted.

However Meditation is not the path to the supreme gift of the Holy Spirit, Agape; contemplation is. Meditation is the raising of the mind to God, contemplation is the raising of the heart. Meditation exposes the yearnings of the heart for God; contemplation is the opening of the yearning heart to meet God in love.

Contemplation is primarily not about what is happening within our selves; it is encountering God and knowing him. Then words fail. Concepts are inadequate. Only the heart is open to God. Jesus instructs us to use all the other forms of prayer that he includes in the 'Our Father', but the prayer that he puts first, contemplation (*hallowed be thy name)*, is the deepest prayer of the heart and we are called to give time to it. We leave aside concerns, worries, thoughts, feelings and stand before God with hearts open. That is how we come to know not about him, but to know him - through love, Agape.

The author of '**The Cloud of Unknowing'** writes:

'God's grace restores our souls and teaches us how to comprehend him (God) through love. He is incomprehensible to the intellect. Even angels know him by loving him. Nobody's mind is powerful enough to grasp who God is. We can only know him by experiencing his love'.[78]

In contemplation we have to enter the cloud of unknowing, set aside emotions and thoughts and images which can never grasp God, and just long for God. Distractions will come and so will deep understandings, but these need to be turned away. Gradually with time and perseverance, the sense of God's love deepens and we become more and more devoted to our Father. Also we begin to experience Jesus' love for everyone. As we progress we can experience dark nights of the senses and also of the soul, but the progression is into deeper and deeper loving union with God. Jesus took Peter, James and John up the mountain of Tabor to witness his glory, but

[78] Butcher C A *The Cloud of Unknowing* (Boston & London Shambhala Publications. Inc. 2009) P 14

when the *'bright cloud'*[79] descended and the Father's voice was heard, they were terrified and fell face down. In his mercy, Jesus treats us more gently. He leads us into the cloud of the mystery of love. This is Agape, the greatest gift of God.

---

[79] Mat: 17: 5

Chapter 10

THE CHRISTIAN HEART

Through Agape, the Holy Spirit releases within us the cry of the child of God: *'Abba, Father!'*[80] St Augustine confesses:

> *"Late have I loved you, Oh Beauty ever old and ever new: late have I loved you. And see, you were within and I was in the external world and sought you there, and in my unlovely state I plunged into those lovely created things which you made. You were with me, and I was not with you. The lovely things kept me far from you, though, if they did not have their existence in you, they did not have any existence at all. You called and cried out loud and shattered my deafness. You were radiant and resplendent, you put to flight my blindness. You were fragrant, and I drew in my breath and now pant after you. I tasted you, and I feel but hunger and thirst for you. You touched me, and I am set on fire to attain the peace which is yours".*[81]

---

[80] Rm 8: 15
[81] His Confessions (Lib. 10, 26. 37-29, 40: CSEL 33, 255-256),

A person who is developing in Agape, becomes more and more a fountain of grace and direction to others. The gifts of the Holy Spirit grow as fruit from their lives: '*love, joy, peace, patience, kindness, goodness, trustfulness, gentleness and self-control*'.[82] How much we strive through our own selves to produce these fruits, and yet they flow from the lovers of God. Jesus teaches us to put our selves humbly before the Father so that our inner selves, our spirits, can emerge.

Agape makes us naked before the Lord and other people. We clad ourselves with so many coverings. Our skin is vulnerable; all of it reacts to touch, especially if that touch is painful; it is the same with our sensitivities. So we work hard at developing a suit of armour to protect ourselves. This may give us a sense of security, but it also increasingly isolates and cripples us, though even the best armours have chinks. From our earliest childhood, our experiences of pain and the failures of love induce us to construct this armour. Bit by bit, with our cooperation, the Father's love unbuckles the different layers of armour, allowing his love, breathing through ours, to cast his light more effectively in our world.

Do not be surprised if he unbuckles it from the inside; the transformation begins in the heart, and only gradually penetrates into our words and deeds. We can see God acting in this way when, on the shore of Galilee, Jesus took Peter aside and three times asked his three times betrayer '*do you love me*'.[83] The third

---

[82] Gal 5: 22
[83] Jn 21; 15

time, Peter humbly, almost tearfully, confesses *'Lord, you know I love you'.*[84] He was being called to an identity different to the strong individual he thought he was. The man, who drew the sword in Gethsemane but then ran away to save his skin, began to be a new creation. He was sensing and choosing a trajectory, the course of which would transform him into one of the dearly beloved lovers of God.

Reality check

God's love gradually enables us to grow. Lovers cannot hide their true selves from each other. That is frightening because, as their brokenness is revealed, they become dependent on the love of the other to aid their healing. Faults which they could not face or fix themselves, their very vulnerability, need the lover's kiss. Sadly, that is often not forthcoming; many lovers turns their face away. God never turns his face away. As his love penetrates the exterior of our hardened hearts, the brokenness of our hearts of flesh emerges bit by bit. It is still frightening, because we can be shocked by recognising wounds and failures which we had not been aware of, or excruciatingly shamed by admitting those we have never been able to fix.

In order to heal and restore us, he will sometimes lead us into wild and frightening places calling us to face the demons that obstruct our way to fuller life. He does not hide the fact that picking up the cross daily is the way forward, but he is right there on that cross with

---

[84] Jn 21:17

us until it is accomplished. Oh, the joy and the peace as we become more free! Western culture idealises the right of every human person to be free, and that usually means permission to do what we want. The freedom God brings about within us is the freedom to be the greatness that we really are. Gradually we are transformed into the utterly unique image of God that each of us is. The life force of God which is gradually released into his servants, his Spirit, moves more freely in us. It is not techniques that we acquire, but life. Bit by bit it dawns on us that there is nothing else worth doing. And the process continues along the long path of becoming *'like stars'*.[85]

Achievements without Agape

If I dedicate my entire life to service, or use my talents superlatively, or bear unimaginable burdens, but am without Agape,[86] I am only working out of a self hidebound by my armour. One day, despite my personal efforts or talents, my energy will dry up. Then I will be left languishing inside my suite of armour. It is dark there and lonely. But, if I have sought the supreme gift of Agape, and walk as one of God's lovers, seeking his face daily, learning to cherish his presence at every step, I do not have to be superhuman or a hero. I will radiate God wherever I am. I will, in the midst of tragedy bring hope, in a broken world bring joy, and in turmoil peace. As I willingly receive the gift of Agape, it will gradually develop me.

---

[85] Dn 12: 3
[86] Cf 1 Cor 12-13

I will not lose my identity as I become a channel of God's love. I will achieve my true identity. The more people see Christ in me, the more they will see the real me where the Lord has helped me to lose the false parts that I thought made me unique and valuable, because I do not need them. **I am unique and valued**. I am one of God's chosen lovers.

I will not be afraid of defeat and failure, because *'all things work together for the good for those who love God'*.[87] Just like on Calvary, all failure will become development.

Huge, even gigantic human efforts will fail to bring about a healed and wholesome world, but the actions of those who are developing in Agape will *'renew the face of the earth'*.[88] The Good News we proclaim introduces people to the truly liberating energy of God, our lover. As we grow into the state of being the beloved children of God, we are revealed as the ones for whom creation is *'waiting with eager longing'*.[89]

As St Paul wrote to them, the Church of Corinth was proud of the wonderful charisms of healing and prophecy and teaching that they were experiencing. How much more would they have fulfilled their mission if they had put Agape at the top of the wish list for divine gifts! It seems that many of them failed to grasp this deepest teaching of Paul, because some forty years

---

[87] Rm 8: 28
[88] Ps 104: 30
[89] Rm 8: 19 (English Standard Version)

later, the fourth pope, St Clement of Rome, wrote them a long letter[90] once more urging them to set aside their divisions. The human heart so often focuses on minimal aspirations rather than daring to hope. I believe that in our strange time, God is calling us to focus more urgently on the highest path to growth, Agape. Christopher Fry expresses it as follows:

> *The human heart can go the lengths of God...*
> *Dark and cold we may be, but this*
> *Is no winter now. The frozen misery*
> *Of centuries breaks, cracks, begins to move;*
> *The thunder is the thunder of the floes,*
> *The thaw, the flood, the upstart Spring.*
>
> *Thank God our time is now when wrong*
> *Comes up to face us everywhere,*
> *Never to leave us till we take*
> *The longest stride of soul men ever took.*
>
> *Affairs are now soul size.*
> *The enterprise is exploration into God.*[91]

The time we live in is enormously important in the process of salvation. Nature and history cry out increasingly and urgently for the human exploration into God. That urgency has been infused into us by God. The heart of the Trinity has opened and burns with desire for union with us.

---

[90] The Epistle of St Clement of Rome (AD 35-99)
[91] Christopher Fry: *A Sleep of Prisoners*

What Agape is not

In our frenzied world of today, a new industry of wellness is emerging. To counteract the obsessive use of media and the hurried pursuit of goals, various ways of stilling ourselves and allowing our souls to breathe are flourishing. These are healthy and helpful, and certainly better than using drugs or alcohol. They might prepare us for contemplation, but mostly they seek to balance our selves so that we can be more in control. They are human techniques that lead us to our selves. Agape leads us to the Father.

It grieves me to see how some Catholic schools embrace these methods, because it is evidence of how we have forsaken the habit of introducing our children to the great tradition of Christian contemplation. Yet I have seen a school staff struck with wonder when the children of a whole primary school assembly went into deep stillness and contemplation. We offer our children the notions of the gifts and fruits of the Holy Spirit, but we should start with Agape. Jesus says of children: *'Let them come to me, for it is to such as these that the kingdom of heaven belongs'.*[92] I would rather have a whole system of guiding people in holiness and the knowledge of God than the most impressive school system. The opinion that I have just expressed implies a revolution in our approach to education in our part of the world which would demand courage and dedication if it were put into practice, but is it not the reason why our Father has sent us into the vineyard?

---

[92] Mt 19: 14

'The Spirit breathes where he will'[93]

Throughout my priestly life, I have been privileged to encounter souls that have been led into deep devotion through many paths such as Eucharistic Adoration, the rosary, praying in tongues and the celebration of the Eucharist, and also through suffering or arduous toil patiently endured. As they have matured, they have become leaven in the dough of this needy world. The lovers of God are all around us, usually hidden, but radiating Agape. I cannot draw a map of how the Holy Spirit flows, but I am sure there is an imperative need to give much more Church time to nurturing the ambition for this highest gift. From Agape all other Church outreaches should flow, and would flow wonderfully.

The Sacraments of Reconciliation and Marriage

A greater emphasis on Agape can throw light on some of our current problems in Catholic practice such as the reluctance of people to avail themselves of the Sacraments of Reconciliation and Marriage. Our practice of the Sacrament of Confession often focuses on human motivation by the cold examination of sins and their opposing virtues to elicit sorrow and a firm desire of amendment. This is necessary in cases of deeply mortal sin. Normally, though, it should be where priest and penitent exercise the sacred art of discerning the movement of God's Spirit in the soul of the person

---

[93] Jn 3:6 (Douai Version)

being reconciled. The Sacrament of Reconciliation is the gracious touch of God for one who is earnestly laying bare their poverty of spirit, to encourage them and draw them more deeply into the kingdom of God.

Reconciliation should be a supremely rich encounter with Agape. The poor woman in the Gospel,[94] who was publicly humiliated as her adultery was cruelly publicised by vicious plotters, did not need stoning, she needed to encounter the divinely loving gaze of the one writing on the ground. Only then would she be set on the path towards sinning no more. The paralysed man[95] lowered through the roof by his friends experienced that same infinite love as Jesus told him his sins were forgiven. It gave him overwhelming relief which contributed to the loosening of his seized-up limbs. I think the greatest surprise for both these people was the realisation that this person understands me; he is like me; he has been through these temptations himself and overcome them, and his love radiates the love of the Father of light who cherishes me and has invincible faith in me.

We read in 1 Corinthians 13

'Love is patient, is kind, does not envy, is not boastful, is not arrogant, is not rude, is not self-seeking, is not irritable, and does not keep a record of wrongs. Love finds no joy in unrighteousness

---

but rejoices in the truth. It bears all things, believes all things, hopes all things, endures all things'.[96]

Do we see this only as a check-list of virtues for us to aspire to? Or do we see this as a description of God himself? The woman accused of adultery and the paralysed man caught a wonderful glimpse of the loving God in the eyes of Christ. They encountered the Father who *'keeps no account of wrongs',* and *'is always ready to excuse, to trust and to hope'*[97] in them. The true healing and strengthening of their *'innermost selves'*[98] had started. The Sacrament of Reconciliation should be prepared for and celebrated in the firm belief that it is another step along the road to perfection.

Similarly, how different a Christian marriage becomes if the couple seek Agape together! The lives of such couples as the parents of St Therese[99] shine out as examples of what the Sacrament of Marriage really achieves. Their faithful love and holiness produced daughters who were saints, one of whom is a Doctor of the Church, a supreme teacher of holiness. Why does our marriage preparation stress human relationships and fail to enlighten couples about what happens to their love when they together seek the face of God above all else?

---

[96] Christian Standard Version
[97] 1 Cor 13: 6
[98] Eph 3: 16
[99] Saints Louis and Zelie Martin,

'Set your hearts on his kingdom first, and on his righteousness, and all these other things will be given you as well'[100]

I wrote elsewhere in this chapter that the transformation (of our lives through Agape) begins in the heart, and only gradually penetrates into our words and deeds. St Catherine of Siena puts it like this:

> *'Truly the Soul's being united with and transformed into him [God] is like fire consuming the dampness in logs. Once the logs are heated through and through, the fire burns and changes them into itself, giving them its own colour and warmth and power. It is just so with us when we look at our Creator and his boundless charity (Agape). We begin to experience the heat of self-knowledge – which consumes all the dampness of our selfish love for ourselves. As the heat increases, we throw ourselves with blazing desire into God's measureless goodness, which we discover within our very selves. We are then sharing in his warmth and in his power'.*[101]

Physical fire consumes and annihilates. The fire of the Holy Spirit does not; it matures and enhances our true selves. The adherents of some religions seek to lose their selves in the ultimate reality of universal

---

[100] Mt 6: 33

[101] Catherine of Siena. St, *Oimere Institute of Mystical Experience Research and Education* [online]
Quoting Carol Lee Flinders in *A Little Book of Women Mystics*
Originally in *The Letters of Catherine of Siena* (4 vols), Letter T137.

consciousness. For Christians, eternal life is all about becoming our true selves through harmonious and full relationships and interplay with God and all creation.

Jesus said: '*Eternal life is this: to know you, the only true God, and Jesus Christ whom you have sent*'.[102] When the Holy Spirit works in us through Agape, we are already wrapped in the dynamic of eternal life here on earth. That is the *'power from on high'*,[103] the deluge which Jesus told his disciples to faithfully await; that alone is the fuel for the commission he gave them to transform the world.

'*Our struggle is… against …the spiritual forces of evil in the heavenly realms*'[104]

This third phase of the Church, the third phase of the spiritual revolution which God is gradually conducting in this world, comes as many fruits of the Spirit are ripening. Countries which have heard the Gospel are experiencing peoples' claiming the right to determine their own destiny, and, as we see in the Putin/Ukraine conflict, those who have usurped power for too long are reacting with brutality. Yet the poor and the meek of neighbouring countries opened their doors to the mothers and children of the conflict. Churches frequently became the focus of practical help. Political leaders were seen visiting services of prayer. At the same time, worried people watch, sensing the dimension of the sacred

---

[102] Jn 17: 3
[103] Lk 23; 49
[104] Eph 6: 12

which, in their comfortable prosperity, they have neglected.

The false optimism of western prosperity with its neglect of the poor is yielding to unease and an opening of eyes to the reality of evil. Those who saw the world through rose tinted glasses are becoming dismayed, and those who claimed the moral high ground while scorning those who disagreed are discovering that both their attitudes and those of their opponents are far from answering the deepest yearnings of humanity. We are entering a time when those countries which have blithely, even methodically, thrown out the message of Christ are going to become more earnest in seeking authenticity. Christianity itself is facing up to and dealing with problems within itself which it has evaded. The stage is being set by God for the Church, renewed through deepening its members' holiness, to offer afresh the message of God's love and salvation.

Political pundits hurry to define the near future as a 'new cold war', but the children of God should see it as a special time in the progress of the spiritual warfare Jesus came to cast upon the earth. The millions of members of the Royal Priesthood should not be captivated by the preachers of dread and futility, but become renewed in the vigour of the Spirit. Maybe we have to resurrect an old word, and recognise that we have to become more deeply *devout*. That word places the emphasis primarily on seeking the face of the Father in contemplation, from which authentic actions for peace and love will flow. These actions are the '*spiritual sacrifices*',[105] the acts of loving service among which prayer and the faithful fulfilling of small duties are the biggest part. It is not major strategies which are the main weapons in the armoury of the children of God. We fire bullets of faithfulness, seldom missiles. God looks after the strategies.

Most of today's wars and conflicts are about securing energy resources to enable people's life styles to prosper. For us Christians, our enabling comes from faith, hope and Agape, powers which God gives to those who '*worship in spirit and in truth*'.[106] In today's many outbreaks of war and violence, the distortion of truth through propaganda is rife. But there is also an alarming eruption of truth distortion in all areas of life. Here again the spiritual warfare with Satan is coming to a head. Polarisation and hatred are weighing down heavily on civilisations that thought themselves advanced and sophisticated. All over the world the dissensions of the early Church of Corinth are being repeated. St Paul's remedy is just as urgently to be sought today: to '*be ambitious*' for the '*way that is better than any*':[107] that is Agape. As we Christians become transformed and gently permeate our world with the fruits of the Spirit, this current critical battle in the spiritual warfare will be won.

[105] 1 Pt 2: 5
[106] Jn 4: 23-24
[107] 1 Cor 12: 31

'Not on this mountain nor in Jerusalem'[108]

The Samaritan woman that Jesus met at the well questioned where true worship is centred. He replied that it is not in a place but in each mind and the heart. So we find that Jesus, during his ministry, *'taught his disciples'*.[109] His teaching opened people's minds, to know the truth about God. That gives rise to *'worship in truth'*.[110] Chapters 6 to 8 suggested how we need to grow in knowledge of the truth of God's revelation. But the knowledge of God cannot stay in the mind. It is only the key to opening the door of the heart to *'worship in spirit'*.[111] *'That is the kind of worshipper God wants'*.[112] Jesus was talking about Agape.

The harvest of love

Jesus told us *'when you see me you see the Father'*.[113] Wherever he went, people instinctively sensed Agape, the love of the Father. So wondrous was the healing personality of Jesus, and so compelling his words that people dropped what they were doing and flocked to him. Their hunger for God moved him to infinite zeal and compassion. Listen to Jesus' reaction as he reflects on the multitudes he attracted:

---

[108] Jn 4: 21
[109] Cf Mk 4:34, Mk 9:31
[110] Jn 4: 23-24
[111] Ibid
[112] Ibid
[113] Jn 14: 9

'And when he saw the crowds he felt sorry for them because they were harassed and dejected, like sheep without a shepherd. Then he said to his disciples, "The harvest is rich but the labourers are few, so ask the Lord of the harvest to send labourers to his harvest". '[114]

A more profound ambition for the divine gift of Agape would dispel much of the confusion we see in the Church today. We are so slow to allow the Holy Spirit to renew our hearts and minds. It is no wonder that zeal is weak for reaping the rich harvest with the Good News. The Holy Spirit is beating on our doors, Jesus and the Father want to make their home with every person on the earth. The harvest is as rich as ever. Why are the labourers so few?

---

[114] Mt 9: 36-38

Chapter 11

SEND LABOURERS TO THE HARVEST[115]

Things have changed radically

Forty five years ago, two priests came from France to the parish where I was a young assistant priest. I proudly showed them the primary and secondary schools, the catholic club, and the youth club. One of them surprised me, because he shook his head sadly and said 'This is like it was in France thirty years ago'. I found myself saying the same recently as I listened to a young and enthusiastic woman describing all of the outreaches in her parish. I said to my pastoral assistant 'that sounds like us thirty years ago when we were first worked together in the parish.' Things have changed radically. We cling to and revamp the programmes we have employed for ages and seek to increase them, but people continue to drift away from the Church and our young people are locked in a culture which has little room for God. Our programmes are not working. One thing that the Covid experience has taught is that we can change our methods when we face the need.

---

[115] Lk 10: 2

The vast majority of Catholic parents want Baptism, First Communion, and Catholic schooling for their children, but they don't want Church. Some recognise the contradiction, but increasingly, most just see themselves as loosely subscribing to a catholic culture which entitles them to these things. The majority of baptised Catholics do not know Jesus personally, and most only pray when they need something that they cannot make happen themselves.

"I have come to bring fire to the earth, and how I wish it were blazing already!"[116]

We are not going to even hear what the Spirit is saying to the Churches if we do not confront these facts. Maybe, we are so busy and overworked keeping things going, that we have little time to face these realities, and just become more and more stuck in a dreadful scenario. Maybe thinking about these things hurts too much and we are afraid of being dragged into hopelessness. But I believe that we are going through a baptism which the Lord greatly desires. This is not the end; this is a new beginning. The second phase of the Church has completed its purpose in our Father's plan. It is about to evolve into a third and more deeply effective phase, taking humanity deeper into the renewing of the image and likeness of God. We are on the way to become more like God. But what is God like?

---

[116] Lk 12: 49

Created in God's image

The definitive and most profound fact about God that Jesus revealed to us is that God is family. God is Trinity, three utterly diverse and perfect persons in infinite love with each other, who only speak the language of love. They create in order to share love and communion. We human beings are at the heart of God's love-energised creation. Yet we constantly act as though we own it, and as though our control makes it function. All the while our true nature, modelled after the image of the Trinity, cries out for loving surrender of self so that we can be made alive by the love of others. We yearn to be like God but we build lives of self-sufficiency instead. This is a woundedness that cuts deep into every one of us, the basic and Original Sin. Only doing God's will on earth as it is done in heaven leads to proper renewing of the face of the earth. Surrendering ourselves in love to God is the cure for Original Sin.

God the Father sent his Son to bring about that cure. Through his glorious surrender to the Father in his passion and death he has removed humanity out of the grip of sin; he has restored our ability to surrender in love and so be open to the divine graces we need to become complete. His lovely Lordship has for two thousand years been gradually leading us into his new and redeemed humanity. He is forming us into his mystical body, his Church. All who give him their trust are being drawn into the community at the heart of the new humanity. And there are many who do not know him explicitly, but sense him and follow him to the best of their ability. He entered into our deep frailty and woundedness so that he can gradually cure them.

A time for healing wounds

God understands and allows for our weakness and our constant failure, but every so often he gives his Church a radical overhaul because, despite much progress, weaknesses and failures need addressing in order to allow more progress. We are in the middle of such an overhaul.

Weaknesses that need addressing

What human weaknesses have impeded the Church in its second phase? Here are a few suggestions:

1. People want to feel good about themselves so they set up moral codes to check themselves against. These are good in themselves, but, in our haste for wisdom, we turn them into laws written in stone which make most people feel failures instead. Morality is a servant of love (Agape) not a substitute for it. When people in the Church are more concerned with morality than with love, they work against the Spirit and the Church atrophies.

2. We feel very uncomfortable with chaos, so we seek certainty. This has engendered huge effort in philosophy and theology, and produced dogmas which aid us in having a grasp of reality. Dogma, the official teaching of the Church, also is a servant of love to enable us to *worship in spirit and in*

truth',[117] and not of grasping reality to enable us to feel in control. Our dogmas, the Church's *Deposit of Faith,* have been elaborated under the guidance of the Spirit over centuries by holy and inspired people, but they are notional entities defining more clearly the unchanging truths of revelation. We have become so good at knowing about the Father and the Son, that we often do not know them – just our ideas about them. And, worse still, we have turned our teaching into the imparting of these concepts instead of helping people encounter the loving God, who alone can restore balance to our lives. It is only when someone knows God that they are consumed by a thirst to know more about him. Otherwise, dogma is turned into a form of intellectual ownership and self-security.

3. The Church needs to feel it is fulfilling its mission, but we can be tempted to measure this by the number of people attending Church instead of by the number of lovers of God being born into Christian life. Filling the pews is not a measure of whether we are faithful to our mission, but people becoming filled with the Spirit of God is. We are not number counters; we are midwives of divine life.

4. When Jesus was transfigured gloriously and Moses and Elijah appeared with him on Mount Tabor,[118] Peter was amazed. He immediately proposed that they build three shelters for the resplendent

---

[117] Jn 4: 24
[118] Mt 17:1–8; Mk 9:2–8; Lk 9:28–36

persons. The answer he received was the awesome cloud of the Father's presence descending and his being told to listen to the Beloved Son.[119] We have this compulsion to rush into immediate action instead of listening properly. In a recent webinar about the Pope's book *'Let Us Dream'*,[120] many committed Catholic participants heard his call to go to the margins and minister and set about discussing how to do this, but there was little real grasp of Francis' partner teaching on synodality. That is not primarily about doing things, but listening in deep love to each other and even more to the Holy Spirit to receive his guidance.

It has to be said about the Church that action has frequently trumped the essential pondering that enabled Mary to listen deeply to the Father of the Beloved Son. In the past the Church has been marked by enormous efforts to serve mankind, but there has been a marked tendency to rely on human will-power and to stagnant and contentious polarisation, instead of pondering in brotherly love until the Spirit shows us the way forward. On reflection it should be no surprise that mounting anxiety about climate change, the recent Covid pandemic, war in Europe, and run-away inflation are stopping us in our tracks. The world is being called to listen. Will the Church enable it to listen

---

[119] Mk 9: 7
[120] Invereigh A. *Let us Dream: The Path to a Better Future; in conversation with Pope Francis* (London: Simon & Schuster UK Ltd 2020)

to God? We have to learn again the skill of Christian listening which will lead us to enable the people of the world to listen to God.

5. When organisations seem less effective than they were, people will usually call for a change of management. At the moment, there is much talk about clerical failures, married priests and women priests. It seems to me that these discussions are about Church management. Is there a danger that, in concentrating such a high percentage of Church discussion time on such issues, we overlook that the real management of God's Church arises through entering into the dynamic of the Holy Trinity?

In the world's experience it is evident that changes of management seldom cure root issues; it is all too often a quick makeover which only temporarily quietens anxieties. It is multiple small advances that truly change cultures in organisations and peoples. The true renewal of the Church will only happen when more and more Catholics are drawn by grace into holiness which leads us to exercise more deeply our royal priesthood. This is not moving to the other end of the spectrum where the church is led by laity in a form of democracy, but it is an essential part of the church's journey that clerics and laity listen together to the Spirit working through the Church and, most importantly, follow God's leadership. It is only by a general deepening of each person's spiritual union with God that the salt of the earth will renew its savour and it will get the management it needs.

Learning from experience

Fixating on Christianity's failures in past centuries is counterproductive unless we learn from them. They are in the hands of our merciful Father. God is neither calling us to focus on past weaknesses nor is he calling us to sink into a masochistic vision of gloom for the future. He has led us into the desert to speak in love to our hearts. Here we discover his comforting confidence. He is more intent on renewing the face of the earth than we can ever guess. He is speaking to the heart of his people, his Church. If we listen we will hear the voice in the gentle breeze and he will reveal the names of those he has chosen to work with us and after us. He asks us to temper our lovely haste for wisdom with patience and to be wary of grandiose plans and rigid certainties. He is with each one of us now and surrounds each with multiple small ways of serving him and loving his children here and now.

All he wants is our love and trust, and we will discover that *'all shall be well; all manner of things shall be well'*.[121] From our small faith-filled acts, he will build a massive work of love, a choir so big that its harmonies will renew the earth. His Spirit hovers over the chaos of the new age and culture which is developing. It is moving more quickly to harvest time than we imagine. The world is weary with mankind's

---

[121] D. Graves Julian of Norwich St, Revelations of Divine Love, 13th Showing D, 1342-1416 in *Christian History Institute*, Article No. 31 [online].

failed attempts at engineering civil life, with the greedy ravaging of mother earth, with love's countless failures. It is sleeping, waiting for the gentle wakening voice of God's children. No one can look at humanity without knowing here is great loveliness and goodness; it only waits to feel the touch of the lovers of God. We must encourage each other to become skilled in the tender ways of touching our brother and sister with the Good News. God knows that the harvest is plentiful and he only waits for us to ask him to send Spirit-filled labourers into the harvest.

Ministering - the vocation of all the Baptised

It is important to not look only for ordained ministers and religious to be the labourers. They have their place in God's plan, but so does each baptised person. Let me give an example of how some lay people have grown in ministry.

I know people who become involved in a Church run organisation expecting to experience a community that was Spirit filled. Instead many found a group of men and women convinced of the excellence of the work they were doing but split into factions. They had looked for community but found conflict. This eventually, leads many to leave feeling very hurt.

But for some, that did not destroy their hope of experiencing Christian community. They found themselves clinging to the positive experiences of goodness that they had recognised, and found a growing awareness that God was truly there all the time despite human failure. Out of all that process has grown an understanding that God works among sinners. They have increasingly understood the Church, and grown into lovers of Christ's Mystical body. With that comes a recognition that they themselves are a shepherd within the Church. Their flock is made up of family, friends, fellow Christians, workmates and people they meet seemingly at random. To all they try to be as Christ is.

If we look for Christ, we will find the busy shepherd who is leading a flock of wayward sheep, intimately nourishing each one to growth. You cannot have Christ unless you find him surrounded by sinners. That is Church. It is necessary to accept this before one can share his role of shepherd. By enduring the stress that this brings, we allow the fountain of living water to spring up from within our very selves.[122] It is the gateway to loving with the divine love which we call Charity (Agape).

Co-workers with Christ

There are many who limit their bond with the Church to being supported in the difficulties of life like a comfort blanket. And indeed that is partly the function of Christ's Church. He calls to himself those who labour and carry heavy burdens so that he can refresh them in his gentle and accepting heart.[123] He shares their burdens with them, but all this is

---

[122] Jn 4: 14
[123] Mt 11; 28

so that they will have time and energy to continue to grow, and to ascend the path of maturity to his Father's glory. He wants to encourage us to pass from being passengers to being active sharers in his work. It is easy to become stuck in the desire for consolation, but comfort blankets can stifle maturity. When the blanket turns sour, it is too easily rejected. His meek and humble heart is not simply a place of refuge; it is the gateway to growth in the wondrous love he shares with the Father. Only wanting to receive is to ignore the invitation of Jesus to enjoy the privilege of entering the dynamism of collaboration in God's work of salvation.

The Church truly comprises all men, women and children on the planet, because all, whether they know it or not, are being shepherded by the Son of God; he is at work in myriad different hidden ways. The visible Church comprises those who have come to a sense of this process by which Christ is developing humanity. And they consciously accept and participate in it through Baptism. But the sense develops. At first it is like the first wobbly steps of an infant, who may think that they have achieved all that walking has to offer, but they have not mastered distance and speed and gracefulness. In reality we are all still in the initial stages of transformation into the divine – that is why we all begin each Mass with an act of recollecting our incompleteness.

Within the visible Church, God gradually brings people to the point of being dedicated to the process of Church. It is not the preserve of ordained ministers and religious, but much, much more of all Christians to be the instruments of God's love in the situations and roles that he leads us into. We truly are '*the salt of the earth*'[124] and '*the light of the world*,'[125] a world so yearning for the light.

---

[124] Mt 5: 13
[125] Mt 5: 14

Chapter 12

SOME OF THE TOOLS
FOR THE HARVESTERS

Christianity brings progress

Over the centuries, countries which have been under the influence of Christianity have led the world in progress: e.g. the ending of gladiatorial murder, educational and hospital development, the abolition of slavery, rational and scientific inquiry leading to industrialisation, and equal rights, to mention a few.

True, there have been evils at every stage: war on an industrial scale: ecological damage and imperialism, for example. But in the whole mix, progress has gradually advanced. It is also true that many of the pioneers of progress have been anti-christian or agnostic, but the general liberation of thought arising from Christianity has encouraged the freedom that allowed them to operate.

The Church is this deep current surging through history by which the Spirit inspires God's people to bring about his Kingdom. We Christians need to understand how the Church effects the world. We need to know how the Church functions within the story of mankind.

In Mark 16:16, Jesus' last instructions before his Ascension are: *'Go out to the whole world; proclaim the Good News to all creation.'* This is the mission which determines the nature of the Church. The Church is God's vast and lengthy project, the force or current which the Holy Spirit directs through the centuries of history. We do not understand what it is finally leading to, but we have to reflect seriously on its process.

When I say we do not understand what it is finally leading to, I stress that we do know that all history is leading to the second coming of Christ and the universal liberation of all creation into the Kingdom of God, but when and how exactly this will occur is what we do not understand. Will Christ come suddenly as a thief in the night or will he come when the Spirit has led us to a world which has been maturing in justice and love? Since we do not have the answer now, it is wise to assume that Jesus commissions us to **work for the development of this earth after the pattern of the Kingdom of God.**

Tools that bring forward the harvest

We must reflect on the process of Christianity bringing progress into the world, which means that we need to understand certain essentials of the Christianising process. If we do, we will be equipped with **tools to work effectively**.

1. **Hope.** There will always be evil done by members of the Church; there will always be *'tares'* among

the *'wheat'*.[126] The Lord of the harvest allows this so that the growth of the wheat may not be compromised. At harvest time the tares will be uprooted and destroyed. There are many instances of evil done by Christians, but these are of two types. The first is that there are faults which are unconscious and inherited from existing cultures. History shows that these are gradually corrected under the enlightenment of the Spirit (e.g. slavery). These first are the 'wheat' growing.

The second type are evils perpetrated by people who claim the name of Christian but are in fact *'wolves in sheep's clothing'*;[127] they are the tares. They act for their own selfish reasons and use the good name of the Church, while having no sense of the grace of God. They are culpably non-christian as their acts show, but they cause scandal in the minds of many and inhibit the work of the Spirit. In every one of these cases, there comes a harvest time when the tares are removed.

We seriously need to reflect on these two phenomena, continually discerning what must be called evil and condemning it, but understanding that many of those involved are part of a genuine movement forwards, while others were abusive, consciously exploiting the Church for their own shoddy purposes. God not only allows this mix, but it seems to have his blessing because he knows

---

[126] Mt 13: 24 - 30
[127] Mt 7: 15

what wheat is made of. People are not born saints, but gradually attain perfection through the progressive correction and gracing of God. If we understand this, we will maintain **hope** – *'all things work together for the good for those who love God'*.[128]

2. **Courage.** Complicated situations are not changed in an instant but gradually over time through well-meaning efforts at advancement, however faulty at first, and always in the face of cruel resistance and even betrayal by those who seemed to be friends. The divine gift of Christian hope is strengthened by understanding how Spirit-inspired progress develops gradually in history, and, from this, another gift of the Spirit comes: **courage**. A wonderful example of this is St Edmund Campion's *'Brag'* where, in 1580, he explained how he dedicated himself to the purifying of Christianity in England: 'The expense is reckoned, the enterprise is begun; it is of God; it cannot be withstood'.[129] **Hope and courage** are essential tools of the Holy Spirit.

3. **The world follows the speakers of truth.** St Matthew expresses the great mission that Christ gave to his Church at his Ascension like this:

> *'Go, therefore, make disciples of all the nations; baptise them in the name of the*

---

[128] Rom 8: 28

[129] E. Campion St, (1781) *Challenge to the Privy Council (Campion's "Brag")*[online] Catholic answers 1994 Catholic cutlure.org No. 8

*Father and of the Son and of the Holy Spirit,
and teach them to observe all the commands
I gave you. And know that I am with you
always; yes, to the end of time'.*[130]

A disciple is one who is being taught, and Jesus
tells us to 'teach' the nations to observe all the
commands he gave, which he summed up as *'love
God and your neighbour as yourself'.*[131] Teaching
is the methodology of the Spirit's re-creation
of the human race. It is necessarily a gradual
process, and all individuals and communities learn
at their own pace, but the teaching will not cease;
it is of God.

Practically, the teaching arises from the Church
always going out ahead in human development.
This trail-blazing is risky as described in a poem of
D H Lawrence entitled *The Prophet:*[132]

*Ah, my darling, when over the purple horizon
shall loom
The shrouded mother of a new idea, men hide
their faces,
Cry out and fend her off, as she seeks her
procreant groom,
Wounding themselves against her, denying her
fecund embraces.*

---

[130] Mt 20: 19-20
[131] Mt 12: 30-31
[132] D. H. Lawrence, *Amores.* New York: B. W. Huebsch, 1916; Bartleby. com, 1999. [online]

In challenging contemporary norms and perceptions, the Church will face persecution, but the Spirit of God will always guide the prophets, even to martyrdom. Usually, the process involves many Christians and other people of good will who are gradually inspired by the prophets and who advance the teaching through word and example. Here it is important to stress the outreaching nature of the Church. Her members are called to be the *'yeast in the dough'*[133] which demands that they thoroughly immerse themselves in human societies and cultures, not cutting themselves off in an isolated attempt at a 'perfect society'.

Teaching is the pathway to educate, which means to draw out potential which is present, and it cannot be done without the risky business of identifying ourselves with the rest of the world just as Jesus identified himself with all of us. One tool which helps us in this mission is the firm **conviction that, reluctantly but ultimately, the world follows the speakers of truth**. The Evil One attempts to discourage the children of God by creating a mind-set that things are too strong to be altered. He uses this tool ingeniously, but the tool God gives his children is the firm conviction that God is directing the process not the devil nor human agencies. What is of God will not be withstood no matter how much time it takes, nor the expense.

---

[133] Mt 13:33; Lk 13:20-21

4. **God raises up allies for his people**. The Church as an institution outwardly has its own organisation and membership, but, as a spiritual reality, it is the epicentre of the awakening of the new creation which involves every human being. All humanity is part of the Church either consciously or without knowing it, because the Church is the Body of the Son of God who joined himself to all mankind at his Incarnation. Her baptised and faithful members are called to seek in all people the image of Christ and to dedicate themselves to loving and serving them until '*Christ be formed*'[134] in them as St Paul says.

When the Angels appeared to the Shepherds at Bethlehem they proclaimed God's purpose of '*Peace on Earth to people of good will*'.[135] They did not say that God directed his peace to those who were conscious of being his chosen people, but to all people of good will. One essential tool of God's people is knowing that, in all movements of the Spirit, God raises up men and women of good will who, while not being Christians outwardly, are co-workers in progressing the work of God on earth. Acts 18: 9-11 tells us how St Paul and St Barnabas worked in Corinth with renewed assurance because

> '*One night the Lord spoke to Paul in a vision*'
> *and said: "Do not be afraid to speak out, nor*

---

[134] Gal 4:19
[135] Lk 2: 14

allow yourself to be silenced: I am with you.
I have so many people on my side in this city
that no one will even attempt to hurt you.'

It is important to remember that **God raises up allies for his people**.

5. **Christians know that God is at work in the life of every person.** There is often among Christians today a false modesty which is embarrassed by the exclusive claim of Christianity that Jesus is the centre of all reality, the only way to God. This seems to be contradicted by so much evidence of good people who do not know Jesus, many of whom are holy and full of charity. That often leads to the commonly stated view today that there are many authentic paths to God and to progress in this world, and that Christianity is only one way among many.

It is all part of the modern philosophy which says that, because there are so many contradictory claims to truth expressed today, it is impossible for us to know ultimate truth. I am sure that this belief springs from many well-meaning people's horror at the violence with which those who hold to different religions and politics often injure and cancel eachother. So they make tolerance the highest virtue. But the superficial peace they seek denies the deep search for wisdom which is in mankind. To achieve tolerance they suppress the search for truth which is at humanity's core. To achieve greyness they cancel the rainbow.

Christ was occasionally angry, such as when he cleared his Father's house to restore it as a house of prayer not commerce. When he challenged the Jewish leaders, he used forthright truth but never used violence. When one of them, Nicodemus, came genuinely seeking, or Pilate seemed to be in earnest, Jesus patiently and respectfully explained the truth, but accepted death and pain instead of inflicting it. He teaches his followers to act in the same way, to expect persecution, but never use it. He revealed the profoundly liberating power of loving one's enemy. True tolerance for us Christians is not avoiding all forms of contradiction, but enduring the pain of differences peacefully and honestly, until full truth emerges. We rely on the gift of *'the peace of God which is so much greater than we can understand'*, [136] and must repudiate any use of violence or coercion.

We believe Jesus with all our hearts when he says *"I am the way and the truth and the life"* [137] and that *"no one can come to the Father except through me"*. [138] We believe that he is the absolute and final self-revelation of God, and that we are commissioned to announce, explain and demonstrate this to the world.

We do not deny that many non-christian *ways* contain great good, nor deny that God is walking

---

[136] Phil: 4: 7

[137] Jn: 14: 16

[138] Jn: 14: 6

with the people involved, and is busy in their lives. Indeed we know that no one can produce the fruits of the Spirit without the help of the Spirit. So God is active and supportive of all people of good will. Furthermore we Christians must affirm that Jesus is walking with them even though they may not know him, because he is the way to God. So their paths are not separate and distinct to the way of Jesus, but just more clouded since the presence of his hand in their lives is obscured. This is equivalent to our understanding that people who reject or live in ignorance of God are still sustained and blessed by him. Likewise, those who do not know that Jesus is '*the Way*'[139] are still on Jesus' Way as they grow and progress. The traditional term for this state is Baptism of Desire. At some time in God's providence, they will become enlightened about Jesus and his Church, since that is the will of God. Christians know that **God is at work in the life of every person.** So we remain positive and hopeful for everyone's salvation.

6. **History progresses as much in little steps as in dramatic ones.** God's work of renewing the face of the earth is, for the most, part done in little steps, but each step draws the enormous human family bit by bit to Christ. Satan is always whispering discouragement to us to torment us into denying that each small step of love and goodness has any value, whereas Christ assures our hearts that

---

[139] Jn 14:16

'*all things work together to the good for those who love God*'.[140]

Christ tells us that '*those who are faithful in little things will be faithful in great*'.[141] The supreme example of this is Mary, who lived in perfect love of God each humble moment of her life as wife and mother, and then so joined herself to her Son on Calvary that she became the new Eve, the Mother of all mankind.

The Spirit endows the children of God with understanding that no prayer, no tear, no drop of sweat, no effort is too small to be used in the '*great act of giving birth*'[142] for which the '*whole of creation has been eagerly awaiting*'.[143] The insight that **history progresses as much in little steps as in dramatic ones** is a vital tool for Christians. These are the normal spiritual sacrifices of the Royal Priesthood.

Into the future using these tools – Ecology and other spheres of action

As other elements of human societies take up the development of education and health care in the West, the Church's presence in these matters has become more supportive and less trail blazing. The question to

---

[140] Rom 8: 28
[141] Lk 16:11
[142] Rom 8:2-23
[143] Rom 8: 2-23

ask is: 'what is the Spirit saying now to the Church?' As usual, he will be calling his children to trail blaze in several directions – God is ever busy. One enormous enterprise is the whole issue of ecology. Here the Church is involved through her members on many different levels, but Pope Francis reminds us to be true prophets, in that we all need to be converted to sharing the world's resources as brothers and sisters. That will necessitate a change of heart in all people, especially those who enjoy wealth and prosperity as we do in the West.

The false philosophy at the heart of much ecological thinking is that a command economy will be necessary to force people to do the right things by creation. This springs from a scepticism about human goodness and is often marked by anger and aggression. That cannot lead to true sharing of the world's resources, since it is framed in the mentality of winners and losers – a contest like Marxism. A protracted process of opening people's hearts to justice and love is the only thing that will bring true and collaborative stewardship of creation. As Christians and people of good will enable this opening, a truly wholesome world can develop, but it will take much time, courage and hope.

Synodality

But there is one area for the Church to be of special service which I would like to highlight. At the moment we are acutely aware of the polarisation of opinions all over the world. It is frightening how much controversy is filling the ether, and how violent and aggressive the proclaiming of opinions has become. The media incessantly feeds this. People are mesmerised by this cacophony into a dull despair that humanity can never attain peace and concord. Pope Francis prophetically points the way forward. His catchword is *Synodality*.

Synodality is a special charism of the Church. Whilst the world tries to settle disputes through diplomacy and politics, or violence if the first two fail, the Lord calls and gifts his Church with the unity which is in the Trinity. This works through Christians speaking the truth as they see it to one another, and listening deeply to each other in a spirit of fraternity. Pope Francis warns us to avoid having '*isolated consciences*'[144] where we hold to our own views against others and limit our communication to those who agree with us.

More than listening deeply to each other in love, Synodality calls us to pray to hear what the Holy Spirit is saying in all the debates. It requires a firm conviction that it is the Spirit who leads the Church, and that taking any other direction than his only leads away from God. When we humbly listen to each other even when we have great divergences of views, and wait for the Holy Spirit to lead, we will always get what the Pope calls *overflow*,[145] a step forward often different to what either side proposes, but which unites and lifts the

---

[144] A. Invereigh *Let us Dream: The Path to a Better Future; in conversation with Pope Francis* (London: Simon & Schuster UK Ltd 2020) pp. 69-73

[145] A. Invereigh *Let us Dream: The Path to a Better Future; in conversation with Pope Francis* (London: Simon & Schuster UK Ltd 2020) pp. 80 ff

debate up into real progress. This process will take time, but compared to the time wasted in forcing and resisting change on the human level, it is rapid. *'Those who wait upon the Lord renew their strength, they put out wings like eagles. They run and do not grow weary, walk and never tire'.*[146]

As I write, the process of preparation for the Synod on Synodality is underway. There are few moments in the life of the Church when a renewal of strength, through waiting upon the Lord, is more crucial. This waiting is not being inactive; it is urgently longing to receive the *overflow* of the Spirit. It is making that longing our heartfelt prayer. We must be like Jacob, after a night of struggling with God, saying: *'I will not let you go until you bless me'.*[147]

So many committed Catholics are weary of past consultations, and distressed or distracted by the media's obsession with issues which polarise the members of Christ's Body. The task of listening to eachother until the inspiration of the Holy Spirit is discerned seems almost too much for our human strength, but not for God who has brought us to this moment.

As the Synod is gathering pace, it is good to remember the question that Jesus posed to the apostles: *'What were you arguing about on the road?'*[148] Their answer was embarrassed silence, because they were

---

[146] Is 40: 31
[147] Gn 32: 28
[148] Mk 9: 33

clashing over their individual importance. He told them to make themselves the least important and everyone's servant, and to welcome his Father in little ones.[149] The ones who serve, wait upon their Lord, and with courage and humility focus attentively on his every breath. Our Lord's breath is not an external collection of words, it is the force of his very being, his Spirit, working in our hearts.

We are not merely a coalition of human beings, but a communion of saints and our repeated failures can never outweigh the determination of the Trinity so clearly expressed in Jesus' last prayer over the Apostles before he went to his death:

> *'I pray for those who through their words will believe in me. May they all be one. Father, may they be one in us, as you are in me and I am in you, so that the world may believe it was you who sent me'.*[150]

Here, Jesus is describing the divine dynamic of Trinity which is the true driving force within his Church. He is calling down the gift of divine unity to bind his members in communion. If we act in a truly synodal way, the Father himself will enable us to hear his voice as he speaks in different ways through all the members of Christ's body. His Spirit is able to make, of many voices, one.

---

[149] Cf Mk 9: 33-37
[150] Jn 17: 20-21

This has an immediate impact on the whole world. If we can allow God to revitalise the sacred charism of synodality, then we can serve our local and global world in its progress towards understanding and collaboration. I, personally, think that millions of Church members who have learnt the listening skills and understand the tools of patiently and painstakingly forging unity under the Spirit's guidance, will offer the world innumerable avenues to peace, and sustain the peace-makers in their vital role. I believe this service will be as great as the Church's past contributions to progress in education and health care.

The Catholic Church already has a vast and effective diplomatic service with embassies in 86 countries and a further 113 Apostolic Nunciatures in others. There, through quiet diplomacy and participation in international bodies, it works for peace and justice. But that is the tip of the iceberg compared to the combined work of reconciliation which all individual Church members are called to do in their families and localities. How much more good would be done if the profile of the charism of synodality is heightened!

SECTION II

THE GOOD NEWS

The Gospel

I wrote in the previous chapter about some of the tools we harvesters have been gifted with so that we may be encouraged to persevere in the service of the Gospel, but the primary tool is the Gospel itself. It is the two edged sword that penetrates people's hearts. Each of us needs to repeatedly hear it anew in order to display it afresh in all the new situations God places us in. It is a jewel with an infinite number of facets, always calling us to continually study it from different angles to see it in fresh light. What I write in this section is offered from my own reflections and preaching of the Good News.

'I bring you news of great joy to be shared by all the people'[151]

St Paul was filled with zeal to bring others to know the Gospel. In 1Corinthians 2, he gives an insight into his method of preaching it. With real *'fear and trembling'*, he proclaimed to people *'the Crucified Christ'*, the *'hidden power'*[152] and *'hidden wisdom of God'*,[153] and that caused many to open the door to the Holy Spirit who then taught them *'to understand the gift God has given us'*.[154] The ancient word for this proclamation of the Good News is **Kerygma**. It enlightens people, moves them to wonder and praise and makes them want to never be the same again.

---

[151] Lk 2: 10
[152] 1 Cor 2: 5
[153] 1 Cor 2: 7
[154] 1 Cor 2: 13

In these next four chapters, I try to share my own excitement, and give some of the Kerygma as I share it with others. I write about the dynamic functioning of our Royal Priesthood, the mystery of human communion, the world changing power of the death of Christ, the depth of our sin-wounded selves being cherished to wholeness by the Father through Jesus, the utter centrality for Eucharist, and the spreading the Good News. Then, in Section III, I deal with the divine explosion of the energy of God which we call *Church*, and the essential part we each have within it.

Chapter 13

THE SPIRITUAL SACRIFICE

The Royal Priestess

Royal Priesthood is lived out in so many ways. Let me introduce you to Samantha and her story. A widow, she was the victim of someone's unscrupulous plan to make money. When she finally pulled the plug, she was out of pocket by a considerable amount. People expect her to brood on it, be bitter and give in to hatred. She is resisting that temptation and the inclination to self-pity. This inner battle to maintain her peace and to be faithful to Jesus' command to love her enemy is a big part of the priesthood she is called to exercise here and now. It is the *'spiritual sacrifice'*[155] that St Peter talks about when he describes those who are part of God's new creation of a *'Royal Priesthood'*.[156]

Does Samantha realise that in fighting the temptations to be swallowed up in negative feelings, she is uniting herself to her saviour on the cross? How much more productive it is to stay close to his suffering heart which is so totally positive, looking Satan straight

---

[155] 1 Pt 2: 5
[156] 1 Pt 2: 9

in the eye until he backs down. Every time Satan backs down, his hideous power is diminished. He will not be as able to undermine other people as efficiently, and the Kingdom of God is advanced. The Royal Priesthood has been effective and the result is that others will be drawn into that Saviour's love.

One of Satan's ploys is to whisper that her patient struggle against bitterness is irrelevant, that she is worthy of doing greater things, more dramatic things, for God. The father of lies is only trying to undermine this greatest thing, this deep but hidden drama, by which she is glorifying God and collaborating in her own purifying and that of all mankind.

'To do what I can to make up all that has still to be undergone by Christ for the sake of his body, the Church'[157]

When St Paul proclaims a *'crucified Christ'*[158] he goes to the heart of salvation warfare. Did Jesus not promise that, when he was *'lifted up from the earth'* he would *'draw all men'* to himself?[159] At the time of his passion, the *'hour of darkness'*,[160] he who *'knew all people'*[161] and *'what was in each person'*,[162] gathered us all into his own heart with our sin and pain, and he summoned

---

[157] Col 1: 24
[158] 1 Cor 2: 2
[159] Jn 12: 32
[160] Cf Lk 22: 53
[161] Jn 2: 24 (New International Version)
[162] Jn 2: 25 (New International Version)

the *'Prince of this World'*[163] to the definitive contest for all mankind. When he finally proclaimed *'It is accomplished'*,[164] and *'Father into your hands I give my spirit'*,[165] he breathed out his spirit in a loud cry. That was the cry of victory. Satan was *'Prince of this world'*[166] no longer. The soaring spirit of the *'Son of Man'*[167] swept redeemed mankind into the Father's embrace. That death, his voluntary leaving of this world, brought humanity back into the heart of the Triune God. The power of death is destroyed and transformed into victory. Now the countless instances of death which we experience throughout our lives are joined to his and become platforms of worship, which transform suffering into redemption. Samantha's struggle is not hers alone but part of the God's whole gigantic tapestry of human redemption.

Jesus had spoken of his utterly unique death in a tense exchange with some Pharisees. After he stated that he was the Good Shepherd, who would lay down his life for his sheep, he then went on to say:

> *'I lay down my life in order to take it up again. No one takes it from me; I lay it down of my own free will, and as it is in my power to lay it down, so it is in my power to take it up again; and this is the command I have been given by my Father'.*[168]

---

163 Jn 14: 30
164 Jn 19:30
165 Lk23:46
166 Jn 14:30
167 Mt 8:20 and Lk 9:58
168 Jn 10; 17-18

Here he explicitly states that he chooses when he will die, and when he will rise again. He had come to fulfil the Father's plan, which was that in the ultimate battle of Calvary he would rally all humanity to himself and wrench us from Satan's domination. Then he would use death itself as the gateway to our sharing in the life of God here on earth, and that sharing would blossom in eternity.

Now death, our worst fear, has become our friend. Despite our dread of it, when, in spiritual sacrifices, we embrace with him instances of dying, seeds of grace and eternal life are sown. We Christians must penetrate to the depth of this mystery of sharing redemption. We must not react to Jesus' words like some of the Jews that Jesus was arguing with: *'Many said "He is possessed, he is raving, why bother to listen to him?"*.[169] But some did listen and so must we. Now, through freely uniting ourselves to the death of Jesus, we join with him in reversing the crazy path of human corruption.

'Father may they be one in us'[170] – the Restoration of Human harmony

We became corrupt as a race through people freely choosing to follow their own plans rather than God's. No one can deny how our choices riddled our nature with wounds. We add to the wounds and pass them on through each generation. In our clouded understanding we keep attempting quick fixes, but they only make

---

[169] Jn 10: 20
[170] Jn 17: 21

things worse and add to the profound trauma in which we feel locked. But we are locked no longer, for Christ's healing explosion of trust has penetrated right to the roots of the trauma, to the regions where we are all connected.

Deep, deep within us his sacrificial love is at play when we call down its power every time we offer *'the Spiritual Sacrifice'*.[171] On the surface of our self-awareness we seem to act alone, but unity is being restored through each good deed, just as it is disrupted by each sin. On the eternal balance sheet, sin is defeated; in the dimension of time its power is mortally wounded and scheduled for destruction. The inexorable victory of Christ and his people is guaranteed.

There are myriad forms of spiritual sacrifice. It may be dedicating time to pondering God's goodness; it may be the heroism of one who persists for years in the painfully demanding caring for another. But all worship is communal. When we are in contact with God, we are in a mystical, real way in communion with all mankind. Humanity is not just a collection of individuals; we are brothers and sisters bonded at incredible depths where the drama of human re-creation is being affected. We will fully realise the amazing interconnectedness of humanity only when we are at home in the glory of heaven. Then we will see how every one of our breaths of love here and now enabled distant souls to awaken or to grow. At present we only sense this mystery of

---

[171] 1 Pt 2: 5

communion, but, with each new act of worship/love, the sense of its reality deepens.

How strenuously Jesus had desired to accomplish the baptism[172] with which we were to be baptised into himself, and so into the communion of the Trinity! With what still greater urgent longing does he wish his new Body, the new humanity, to transform the whole world into unity! As he wept over the obstinacy of Jerusalem, he agonises over our recurrent failure to acknowledge our dignity, to truly let flow the supernatural life urgent to stream through us. Christ's agonising is no despair; as he once set his face firmly towards Jerusalem, he now is in our midst operating firmly on his knowledge that all '*is accomplished*'.[173] If necessary, he will not hesitate to shatter our complacency in order to revive his people's willingness to '*offer the Spiritual Sacrifices*'[174] which will release the flow of his Spirit into this new age.

We proclaim your death, Lord Jesus

The word 'sacrifice' can seem uncomfortable to our pleasure-seeking age. It is like Lent which can also come across as negative. Is there about Lent a silent recognition that we should be miserable at that time – maybe, so that we will rejoice with relief at Easter? Is this mentality a close ally to many people's uncomfortableness when we say: "*We proclaim your death until you come*"? How come Jesus' death is something to proclaim? Is it because

---

[172] Lk 12: 50
[173] Jn 19: 30
[174] 1 Pt 2: 5

it is the greatest drama of all time, the supreme example of super-human courage? Is it not rather because the voluntary death of Jesus is the most pivotal, positive and brilliant event of human history? It was not an end of a life, but the complete joining of human life to heaven. What seemed defeat on Friday shone forth as victory at Easter.

It is hard to comprehend the enormity of the victory of Christ's death

I felt the weight of suffering when I watched the Good Friday Stations of the Cross from Rome. It was composed by prisoners, many of whom were disadvantaged from childhood. It was a heart rending insight into the suffering, brutality and remorse of prisoners. I was just stunned by their pain in experiencing sheer evil. The year before it was led by migrants and refugees who had seen friends drowned at sea or languishing in internment camps. I know I cannot comprehend the vastness of human pain caused by evil committed, suffered and inflicted. I am capable of only briefly contemplating the hideous faces of sin. I know all evil has an end, but I could never imagine its monstrous enormity. Even if I invited all evil into myself and writhed on the ground in agony, I could not really experience it in its totality. Only one person has tasted and grasped it all: the one who sweated blood in Gethsemane.

How can I comprehend the infinity of God's mercy if I cannot imagine the finite vastness of evil? The two came up against each other in the heart of the crucified,

I cannot comprehend it. There, as that fully developed, perfect man drew all of mankind into himself, through and in him, humanity finally threw itself with complete confidence into the heart of the Father. And, as Christ fully expected, we were healed by our Father, the only one who can convert all evil into glory, and the Father did this with infinite compassion. Had he not proclaimed his pleasure as he saw Jesus embrace and own our sin in the Jordan? Mercy has conquered, and the power of sin and death is defeated. Truly, all was *'accomplished'* on that **Good** Friday. There is nothing better to proclaim than the mystery of that wondrous, victorious death which started our journey to everlasting life. That death is the gate through which we redeemed sinners arrive home.

Chapter 14

MERCY WITHIN MERCY
WITHIN MERCY

When asked to define himself, Pope Francis answered: *'as a sinner'*.[175] How profoundly he put his finger on what we all are! Again and again I myself sully the image of God in my own being. Then I can be crippled by self-disgust and the discouragement that whispers I will never change. If I accept this narrative of myself, I will have given up, and allowed myself to be gripped by despair, the unforgivable sin. It is unforgivable because forgiveness is simply not sought. Mercy stands knocking at the door and I will not answer, because I am tired of this continual experience of self-loathing. I just want to stop caring.

In my shallowness and hurt pride I am totally unaware of the enormity of my being and how profoundly wounded I am. I obsess about a few of my failings, while being ignorant of the deep chasms of unfulfilled being within myself which need touching, healing and filling. I complain 'why don't you fix this in me?', while he is busily at work in my innermost

---

[175] A. Spadaro, (SJ) *A Big Heart Open to God: An interview with Pope Francis in* America the Jesuit Review (2013) [online]

being. How easily I convince myself that I know what I need more than he does! He concentrates on the root causes, while I obsess about the symptoms.

Sometimes I have glimpsed my God-given beauty and what I am capable of under his guidance, but that often makes me more deeply disappointed each time I sin. May I never forget the maxim: *'where sin abounded, grace did more abound'*.[176] Mercy after mercy lines up before and behind me, more than I can ever have need of. I need love, I need nursing, and I need understanding. I need to be trusted until I can believe in myself. Only God does all this; even my sin is turned to the good when I turn again to the love of Christ. There is nothing sweeter than that tender mercy, no more effective balm for the soul, nothing more encouraging than Jesus' assuring call to take up the yoke with him again. I will only stop obsessing about my self-image when I discover the image of myself that is reflected from his fond eyes. We are made in his image, so at the heart of our being we are designed to be the most beautiful and amazing creatures. God is busy at work in each one of us until we *'shine like stars for all eternity'*.[177]

How blinkered we are when we focus too much on our own capabilities rather than the immense power of God! It is so restricting to rely mostly on human endeavour rather than looking to the King whose Spirit nurtures the true fruits in growing souls. Catholics

---

[176] Rom 5: 20
[177] Dn 12: 3 ; Mt 13:43 (like the sun),

must first confess the deeply active mercy of God before they can properly confess their sins and touch deeply the ever-flowing consolation and absolution of the Crucified heart of Christ. The Church has always taught that a perfect act of contrition guarantees absolution, which perplexes us because we think that means that we have to attain a deep level of sorrow for causing Christ to suffer. Really, it means penetrating through all our notions of Christ to glimpse the blazing love of his heart. Then forgiveness is experienced. All other acts of contrition are imperfect. The sacrament of Reconciliation covers the deficiencies of imperfect contrition, but it is meant to lead us gradually to perfect contrition.

God has not stopped cooking us yet! As we progress to glory yoked to him in the protracted uphill pulling, we will fall again and again, and mercy will always be there to lift us up to start again. Each new start is progress! The lovely haste for perfection that is in mankind should not be allowed to obscure the long-haul nature of our ascent into glory beyond our imagining. Together as we involve ourselves more deeply in the sacrificial love of Jesus, humanity progresses.

Chapter 15

A THANKSGIVING SACRIFICE
I WILL MAKE

Gerard Manley Hopkins writes: '*The world is charged with the grandeur of God'.*[178] The experience of natural beauty takes our breath away, so does gazing into the microscope's ever expanding depths. This wonder that is in our DNA comes to maturity when our hearts throb with awe and we worship the God who inhabits all creation.

'*The Holy Ghost'* (Spirit), who '*broods with warm breast and... bright wings'*[179] over the World, sings in the hearts of the Royal Priesthood, often in sighs that '*can never be put into words'.*[180] In the journey of prayer, each soul opens steadily to the joy and the glory of God, letting the Spirit's song emerge. Fundamentally, that song is the sacrifice of thanksgiving, wonder and praise, but, oh, how hard it is to praise! Why does God not make it easier? Because he abhors compulsion and compulsion murders love.

---

[178] G.M. Hopkins *God's Grandeur* in Gerard Manley Hopkins: Poems and Prose (Penguin Classics, 1985) [online]
[179] Ibid
[180] Rom 8: 27

Our God Invites

Think of Adam and Eve; they were obviously not finished but on a steep learning curve. They were to have children who would start as babies and grow to be *'like stars'*.[181] Gradual developers - that is what we human beings are.

Developing can be either passive or active, but it should be a combination of both. We would not do honour to the image and likeness of God in which we are made if we were merely passive. At the same time, we spoil that image and likeness if we are merely active.

The dynamic of the life of the Trinity is collaboration freely exercised. Our true likeness to God shines out as we freely cooperate with him in our own development and the development of all creation. In the steps and stages of our growth, the Father is constantly asking for our consent. The Divine dream for us is spectacular beyond our imagining. He has too high a regard for us to compel us to praise him. God is love, and true love consists in continually committing and receiving. He calls, he waits, and delights when men and women take up the invitation, accept his yoke, and learn from him, the source of infinite bounty. He is not afraid to be 'meek and humble of heart'.[182] Only when we freely collaborate with God does the beautiful free gift of the new creation spread.

---

[181] Dn 12: 3 ; Mt 13:43 (like the sun),
[182] Mt 11: 29

The Human Delight in Giving

Collaborating with God can often feel like plodding, even grueling, service, but it cannot last if there is not the underlying sense of making a gift to the beloved. The joy of giving a present comes because the item given expresses love which cannot be put into words. Love is the mysterious vulnerability and generosity that makes us like God. It needs to overflow into celebration, in ceremonies that use rich symbols. In the Old Covenant God prescribed how the ceremonies were to be enacted. They usually involved sacrifices: the giving of a gift and the sharing of a meal.

Under the Old Covenant, there were different sacrifices for different reasons. Some Jewish Rabbis have taught that, in the last (the messianic) age there would only be the Sacrifice of Thanksgiving. Why in our crazy world should we be confined to thanksgiving? Well, it isn't a crazy world, it's a world full of meaning. Craziness is where the meaning is obscured.

Eucharist

The meaning became obscured at the very beginning. Human beings were created as Royal Priests. At the Fall they lost this when they gave in to the temptation to *'become like gods'*.[183] What a con! They were already the image of God, who was nurturing them towards full-grown glory. It is a simple truth that, since then, all of us have tried to create our own glory,

---

[183] Gn 3: 5

usually with dismal effects. But on the cross, Jesus drank the overflowing chalice of human iniquity and error, taking it into himself and quenching it through his total openness to the Father's healing love. True, for a while he had to hold on with immense fierceness when he felt abandoned, but at that moment of utter surrender and trust, human wilfulness was negated. From his pierced heart flowed out the cleansing water of Baptism, humanities' new birth; and the blood of the Eucharist flowed down his body.

Eucharist means *thanksgiving*. Becoming more aware of God's wondrous love moves us to joyful appreciation which takes the form of thanks, praise and adoration. The Eucharist is the definitive worship of this last age when the love of God is penetrating humanity. It is the assumption of human worship into the liturgy of heaven. The Letter to the Hebrews makes this clear when it says:

> *'Brothers, through the blood of Jesus we have the right to enter the sanctuary (of Heaven), by a new way which he has opened for us, a living opening through the curtain, that is to say, his body... So as we go in, let us be sincere in heart and filled with faith... Do not stay away from the meetings of the community, as some do, but encourage each other to go'.*[184]

---

[184] Heb 10:19-25

The natural human instinct of worship, praise and thanksgiving became separated from the Holy Spirit's heavenly song of creation at the fall of Adam and Eve, and was buried under the heavy layers of corrupted humanity. Man-made religions attempted to cater for this instinctive need, but, in reality, only God-made religion can satisfy. Now, the Spirit's song of creation which is the overflow of the love between Father and Son, has gushed from the cross. It sweeps into itself those who offer the spiritual sacrifices of Trinity love. Each instance of spiritual sacrifice adds to the massive flood of humanity carried by grace. Jesus prescribed the Eucharist as the way of celebrating the mighty current of Trinitarian love. Heaven and Calvary become present in mysterious reality; that is in a way that cannot be put into words.

The Eucharistic celebration lifts us up into the heavenly love affair of the Trinity, whether in the mysterious splendour of a basilica, or the starkness of the gulag, where wine made from smuggled-in raisins, and stale bread made the wonder of the cross and resurrection present in the midst of huddled and emaciated prisoners. The Eucharist is heaven and earth united.

It is the *'source and summit of the Church's life'*.[185] Source because it nourishes the pilgrim. Summit because it is also, in unfathomable mystery, the pilgrim's destination.

---

[185] Paul VI, Pope St, (1964) *Lumen Gentium* [online]. Rome. Holy See No. 11

Chapter 16

GOOD NEWS TO ALL CREATION

The story of my life is one of more or less wilfully following Jesus and more or less accepting his help. I alternate between reluctance to admit that I need his kind mercy, and helplessly falling back into his loving arms. My morbid self-sufficiency battles with my hunger for the life force that only love can produce in me. Poor though I am at accepting his company, I know I have the grace of being aware of it and greatly hope that I will increasingly collaborate with him. If this is the real story of my life, why don't I see that it is the same for everyone? I sincerely hope for the best for me, a sinner. Why do I not expect the same for everybody more keenly? I have seen so many people's need to change, and I have tried to help them change with seemingly little success. There is so much wrong, and people keep repeating it, so I shield my disappointed heart in forgetful indifference or even worse in condemnation. I lack trust in God for whom everything is possible.

If I am really convinced that God never gives up on me, why am I not equally convinced that he never gives up on even the most hardened sinner? Jesus sought out sinners to eat and live with them. Their sin sorrowed him and moved him to ever more expressive love. The only time he was angry was when people turned the meeting place with God into a business opportunity.[186] The only ones he roundly condemned were the ones who hijacked the way to God in order to build their petty bailiwicks. He had no patience with barriers to the Father's love. The more people sinned, the more he cherished them. Truly, *'where sin abounded, grace did more abound!'*[187] He has the same good plans for everyone as for me.

The Father walks into our evening as he did in Eden looking for Adam and Eve,[188] the beloved children he has created in his own likeness. He never stops calling *'Adam where are you? Eve, where are you?'*[189] He has even sent his Son to restore to us his image and likeness. How can I not let that same love consume me? How can I not see that he is sending me as well? My Royal Priesthood is not limited to joining in the song of creation, but is most God-like when I approach each person praying *'Adam where are you? Eve where are you?'*[190] What is stopping me from doing this? What is stopping us?

---

186 Mt 21:12–17; Mk 11:15–19; Lk 19:45–48; Jn 2:13–16
187 Rom 5: 20
188 Gn 3: 8
189 Gn 3: 9
190 Gn 3: 9

SECTION III

EVER OLD AND EVER NEW

Chapter 17

GOD RENEWS HIS CHURCH IN EVERY AGE

When is your birthday?

On that wondrous Easter evening, He who is the Resurrection and the Life comes slipping through their battened door. Calming their alarm and taking little notice of their confused amazement, he breathes on them his gift of the Spirit.[191] It is going to take fifty more days of his teaching and their humble expectant prayer for them to realise what he has done. The breath of God enters poor fallen humanity - our ascent into God has started. They say Pentecost is the birthday of the Church, but we were really born when the soldier's lance opened the vast heart of the Crucified. His new incarnation, his Church received its life-giving Spirit from his very breath on Easter eve, and began to be self-aware at Pentecost.

The Divine Ingathering of Humanity

Before he enters the final battle, Jesus washes their feet and talks to them of love. He even offers a friendship

---

[191] Jn 20: 22-23

token to his betrayer and covers Judas' furtive exit with a gentle word of advice. Then he opens his heart to his friends, revealing his deepest prayer that they be one. This is not an urging upon them of a fundamental strategy. It is the revelation that the utter oneness that he has with his Father is about to replace their frail teamwork with the supernatural power to be one.

His New Commandment of love is not chiselled in cold stone like the old Law; it is the revelation that the totally personal Spirit of God will come upon them individually and communally, empowering them to love one another as he loves. Through the mystery of this gathering of humanity (Church), he will lift them out of this fallen world's disorder into the divine love and unity of the Godhead. Three diverse persons utterly united in perfect, endlessly creative love is the God he reveals. The Spirit, who is that glorious interplay of self-giving and wholehearted receiving between Father and Son, which is so beyond our comprehension, is knocking at the doors of all people, wishing to enter them, to make them one – Jesus only prays that they will be open to it, willingly accept it, and be transformed into the Divine Gathering of Humanity, his new Body: his Church.

'Do not be afraid, little flock. It has pleased the Father to give you the kingdom'[192]

In the previous Chapter, I wondered about our slowness to identify the image of God in ourselves and everyone

---

[192] Lk 12: 32

we meet. I asked: "What is stopping me? What is stopping us?"

Maybe some of this immobility is because we have been shocked by painful experiences. Hopkins sees a little girl's dismay because autumn leaves are dying and he writes: '*Margaret, are you grieving over Goldengrove unleafing?*'[193] He ends the poem with these words: '*It is Margaret you mourn for*'. Today many of us are grieving for the Church we love. The shrinkage, the uncovering of scandals, the accusations of irrelevance, clericalism and so much more rise up to taunt us. Because this does not look like the Church we felt at home in, must we be sorry for ourselves and downhearted and mesmerised by Satan's bellowing a litany of failure and decline?

A short study of the Church's history would soon reveal that we are in a familiar moment in its life cycle. God is cleansing his Church which is '*always in need of being purified, always follows the way of penance and renewal*'.[194] Leaves fall because they are being replaced by buds and shoots that contain more abundant growth. If we took seriously God's determination that everybody has life, we would cast off the garb of mourning.

In previous times like ours, God gifted saints with lively hope. In 1580, at one of the worst moments of

[193] G.M. Hopkins *Spring and Fall* in Gerard Manley Hopkins: Poems and Prose (Penguin Classics, 1985) [online]

[194] Paul VI, Pope St, (1964) *Lumen Gentium* [online]. Rome. Holy See No. 8

religious turmoil, Edmund Campion was afire with hope for religious renewal in England. He returned from abroad to danger, imprisonment and martyrdom two years later at Tyburn.[195] He wrote this to his beloved country:

> *'We are willing cheerfully to carry the cross you shall lay upon us, and never to despair your recovery, while we have a man left to enjoy your Tyburn, or to be racked with your torments, or consumed with your prisons. The expense is reckoned, the enterprise is begun; it is of God, it cannot be withstood. So the Faith was planted: so it must be restored'.*[196]

Campion's hope is as fresh as ever in our own time of turmoil. The Faith that has so often been planted and replanted in blood, sweat and tears is urgent for its own renewal.

Sailing in a sea of change

In my childhood and youth I experienced a Church greatly convinced of its own rightness, defining itself as 'a Perfect Society', tightly organising every stage of life and confident in its large numbers. Catholic Foreign Missions were almost over-run by people seeking Baptism, and here we prayed confidently for

---

[195] Tyburn: near present day Marble Arch, was for over 650 years the principle place of execution in London.
[196] E. Campion St, (1581) *Challenge to the Privy Council (Campion's "Brag")*[online] Catholic answers 1994 Catholic cutlure.org No. 8

the Conversion of England. It has to be admitted that this gave many of us a strong sense of security and identity. There was no lack of people coming forward to be priests and religious. The Parish Priest where I was ordained, a lovely man, told me in his speech at my ordination reception that "You have just joined the best club in the world". Even as a newly ordained greenhorn, this disturbed me. It might have been partly because I was a priest trained during the Second Vatican Council, albeit with a rather imperfect grasp of its teaching and message. I already sensed that priesthood is not some privileged and exclusive closed shop, but a vocation to serve. Imperfectly, I, like many others, was sensing the shifting of tectonic plates in the Church.

Only six years later (1975), Pope Saint Paul VI was pointing to a changing atmosphere in the Church. He spoke of

'The lack of fervour which is all the more serious because it comes from within. It is manifested in fatigue, disenchantment, compromise, lack of interest and above all lack of joy and hope'.[197]

Pope St John Paul II quoted the above in 1990 when this process had increased, but he wrote:

'Internal and external difficulties must not make us pessimistic or inactive. What counts, here as in every area of Christian life, is the confidence that

---

[197] Paul VI, Pope St, (1975) *Evangelii Nuntiandi* [online]. Rome. Holy See No. 80

comes from faith, from the certainty that it is not we who are the principal agents of the Church's mission, but Jesus Christ and his Spirit'.[198]

I have been a priest for over 53 years and have played my part in the whole process by participating and coping with the changes. Throughout it all, I have maintained a great respect for my fellow priests and feel that the vast majority of us have genuinely tried to cope with the enormous change in our culture and the Church's reforms. It has not been easy. It has not been easy for all faithful and concerned Catholics. What has sustained my hope and made it grow is a message I heard as a young priest. I believe it was a message for its own time and that time is rapidly approaching.

---

[198] Paul VI, Pope St, (1979) *Redemptor Hominis* [online]. Rome. Holy See No.36

Chapter 18

A MESSAGE FOR ITS OWN TIME

Mary

Forty eight years ago, an older lady named Mary, whom I took seriously, came and told me Jesus had appeared to her. He was sorrowing and, when she asked what was the matter, he said: "I can't get through my Church. I can't get through my priests". He told her that he was going to shake everything and all would be exposed. He said that then people would come seeking and we have to prepare to welcome them. I still take this message seriously.

For a short time afterwards, I listened to Mary explaining what she had learnt from the Lord about Divine Love. That greatly expanded my understanding and convinced me that here was something genuine. She told me that Jesus had told her to give this **message**[199] to me, and I have wondered what that meant.

About the same time, I was given Habakkuk 2 to read by a friend who stressed that it is a personal message to me. The text has echoed in my mind for the

---

[199] My bold lettering

past four decades, and I still feel it personally. The prophet stands on his watchtower to see what the Lord has to say in answer to his complaint and receives this message:

> *'Write the vision down, inscribe it on tablets to be easily read,*
> *since this vision is **for its own time**[200] only.*
> *Eager for its own fulfilment, it does not deceive;*
> *if it comes slowly, wait, for come it will, without fail'.*[201]

Now, as I write, I offer these thoughts as **'A Message for its own Time'**, the title of this book. Since God is in charge of this whole moment in the Church, I believe that he is completely capable of fulfilling the second part of Mary's prediction of drawing the people to seek him in the Church, and I have offered our thoughts on how we are to prepare to receive them. Certainly the first part of the prediction Mary made that God was going to shake his 'Church and everything' and 'reveal all' is being abundantly fulfilled.

Mary reported that she had been told that, after the shaking, the people would come seeking. I think that the shaking has progressed a long way. But the time when the people would come seeking may still depend on when we are ready to receive the seekers, and I do not think we are. That is why we have stressed that deeper prayer of the heart, and a '*spiritual revolution of*

---

[200] My bold lettering
[201] Hab 2: 2-3

our minds',[202] are necessary for clergy and committed lay people in order to minister properly to the seekers. We believe that it is urgently necessary to assist people in parish groups, to think out together what Jesus's centrality means in their lives. The conversion of heart and minds of individuals and local parish groups must be the real heart of the new development that is to come.

"I can't get through my Church; I can't get through my priests"

In the 1950s there was the beginning of a seismic change in western culture, where everything would be challenged and change; often openly antichristian views would prevail. I see now that in 1962 God gave us the Vatican Council to equip his Church for her mission in the new age which was being born, and which he sees as so rich in redemptive potential. We are half a century into this huge evolution, a lifetime to me, but a short time in the story of God's journey with his people. If there is one thing Church history teaches us, it is that God patiently brings about development and reform in his Church through gradual interplay with all the individuals concerned. The process is always messy, and it sometimes seems that he is asleep in the boat, but he is firmly in command of the storm.

Good and highly motivated Catholics, each of whom has their own take on where the Church is or should be going, will naturally scrutinise the men at the rudder

---

[202] Eph 4: 23

and should not be surprised to find them struggling human beings like themselves. I think that most try to be critical friends, but bishops and priests and deacons are the objects of enormous expectations, and most are their own strongest critics. I hope I don't sound partisan, but I have an enormous respect for my brother clergy who try to follow the Lord in this time to the best of their ability.

Whether as husbands or wives, children or adults, employed or employers, priests or laity it is the expectations placed upon us and that we accept which define how we attempt to fulfil our role, and when circumstances change we try (often slowly) to adapt our roles. In a time of busy harvesting, we decide things quickly and often realise later that we made mistakes. In a time of pruning, a slip of the knife can have disastrous effects, especially if it is you that is being pruned. I certainly have made mistakes which I regret greatly, but I know that, under the mightily hand of God, my genuine errors will be turned to good and they will not prevent his purpose from being fulfilled.

Change does happen

It is expectations which largely inform our actions. I will give two instances of these. Firstly, like most priests, I have baptised thousands of babies, but only gradually come to see that it is the faith of the parents which is crucial for that divine life to grow. Recently, I have postponed baptisms looking for some evidence that parents are trying to be part of the Church. I have done this with a painstaking attempt to be loving and understanding, and mostly with success. Just a few have taken offence and not returned.

Secondly, we had a bad experience with a group of parents of First Communion children, who took to Facebook expressing their anger that they should be required to attend meetings and come to participate in the Mass. This finally persuaded my Pastoral Assistant and I to precede the stage of admitting children onto our next sacramental programmes with a series of discussion/ learning meals for their parents, which was wonderfully facilitated by the parish Evangelisation Team. Some parents opted out, but among those who came there was a perceptible deepening of faith. Only after this course did we accept their children for the Sacramental Programme.

I know that such stratagems are controversial, because of the power of customary practice and expectations, but I believe that there is a growing acceptance among my fellow priests that our approach to the Sacraments of Initiation is not working, and this will shortly lead to a change. Change does happen, but in God's time not ours.

Change is a gradual process

Another lesson from Church history is that it is the people who go ahead and innovate who initiate change. They will either be mistaken or prophets of God. Only time and the Church's discernment validate their actions. Where they are guided by God, the Church follows, but their path will usually have been strewn with controversy and pain. Consensus emerges under the guidance of the Holy Spirit who works in countless members of the Church both clerical and lay. Here Synodality is central.

In fact, I believe that no great reforms have happened without vigorous participation by the laity. Even the Second Vatican Council, where the teachings of the forward thinkers of the previous century were adopted courageously by the Bishops, is only now approaching maturity throughout the whole of the Church. It is certainly not finished, but it *'is of God; it cannot be withstood'*.[203] It would be a terrible blunder for people at this time to focus on the limitations of the clergy in whom the grace of God is still at work. No matter what others do, each of us, clergy and laity alike, are called to sharpen our own efforts to contribute to the great work the Lord is doing in our day. Each of us must focus first on our own continual conversion of heart and mind in order to join effectively in God's process of authentic human development that is his Church.

The danger of Anger

Many faithful Catholics feel frustrated at the pace of change in the Church. They also feel that their talents are unrecognised and undervalued by the clergy. But I would suggest they ask themselves, what plans they have for themselves to give those around them the reason for their hope - do they even find hope in their

---

[203] E. Campion St, (1581) *Challenge to the Privy Council (Campion's "Brag")*[online] Catholic answers 1994 Catholic cutlure.org No. 8

own hearts; do they feel confident and aware of the treasures of their faith; how do they realistically plan to bring young people to God - have they done this effectively with their own grown-up children; do they find their hearts burning within them as God speaks to us in the scriptures; are they angry at Church leaders and complacent about their own ongoing conversion? Is it time that we listened to the words God spoke to Jonah: '*Jonah, are you right to be angry?* '[204]

So many thoughtful Catholics have told me of past initiatives in the Church which they embraced enthusiastically only to find that they seemed to become blocked, or petered out. They are like St Peter responding to Jesus when he is asked to go out again and fish after a hard night catching nothing. Their experiences have left them without much hope for improvement in the Church. May I make two observations?

Firstly, if they look back to the aspirations they had at those times of hope, is it possible that some of them have been advanced without them noticing it? Also what has happened to those who were blocking progress - are they as numerous or as powerful in their positions? Was there a general sense that things could never change because most people seemed unwilling to move - is that as strong? Is there not a much more widespread recognition that change is necessary, even if there is as yet no agreement about the nature of the changes? Is it possible that in all of the huge community

---

[204] Jon 4: 9

of the Church, God is quietly at work, and that he is at work in millions of people?

People frequently say that the laity are not listened to by the Church, yet Pope Francis, initiating the *Synod on Synodality'*, says that we must all, clergy and laity, listen to each other. Could you imagine this happening sixty or even twenty years ago? The Church is moving forward. It will do so wonderfully if we seek to listen to the Holy Spirit above all. If we do, one thing is certain: the Father, who sent his only begotten Son to redeem the world through birth in a humble stable, death on a cross, and mind-blowing resurrection, will surprise us.

Secondly, bear in mind how in past ages God's plan has unfolded gradually, as the people of faith have held on to their trust and hope in him. Look at the development of God's people in the Old Testament. While a decade of our time seems long to us, the history of God's dealing with his people shows that over time there is an inexorable movement forward. While we may hope for a tsunami, the method of God is much more an unstoppable seeping of his actions through multiple fissures in human stubbornness. These will become blocked at times, but God always finds other ways for the rising tide of his will and grace to cover the earth.

Clergy are also frustrated and uncertain. They are very aware of the worries and concerns of their people, which are hard to deal with as they themselves are swamped with all the things required of them. Imagine what it was like for them, to be constantly playing covid-catchup with the ever changing rules for worship and pastoral care during the recent pandemic.

Listening in a lonely place

But maybe the Coronavirus pandemic has really been a gift from God. Maybe he is saying to all his people: "You know you are overwhelmed and things are not really working. See, it is possible to stop and come aside to a lonely place to let me minister to you. You really do have time". The third phase of his Church is beginning. Before we are ready to set out on the journey into the blessings of the coming age, maybe, God has painted the lintels of our doors with protection, enabling us to take time and space to prepare. He has been busy preparing us in more ways than we think. For example, we often worry about the preponderance of the grey haired generation in Church, but they are in fact the watchmen, chosen to remain prayerfully on duty through the dark until dawn comes.

At times like this, keeping busy can be the enemy. Peter wanted to get busy building three shelters in the glory of the Tabor mountain top, while the Father was sending his Son down to Jerusalem to initiate the new creation. His message to Jesus' friends was *'Listen to him'.*[205] Frustration agitates us to want to do something, but the things we feel frustrated about are often merely symptoms of a deeper and more complex malaise. Isn't it time we pulled back on our assumptions and

---

[205] Mt 17: 5

endeavour communally to *'hear what the Spirit is saying to the Churches?'*[206]

One man who listened to the Lord in a lonely place was Pope Benedict in his retirement. In a recent published conversation,[207] he shared his misgivings about the Church in his native Germany. Since the war, it has become wealthy due to a tax levied and donated to the mainstream Churches. That has led to many good developments, but Benedict lamented that, in his opinion, there is an increasing institutionalisation of the Catholic Church in Germany, making it a functional entity rather than the living body of Christ.

He said that *'many of the functions relating to the structure and life in the church were performed by people who by no means shared the faith of the church.'*[208] Because of this, the Church's testimony *'must appear questionable in many ways,'*[209] he said, noting that faith and disbelief *'were mixed together in a strange way',*[210] and 'this had to come out at some point and cause a breakdown that would eventually bury the faith.'[211] Benedict said that in his view, *'a divorce was necessary,'*[212] between these conflicting beliefs. In a brief note, Benedict emphasises that he is

---

[206] Rev 3: 22

[207] Pope Benedict XVI & TobiasWinstel "War Ich ein guter Seelsorger? In *Herder Korrespondenz,August 2021* [online]

[208] Ibid ., p 8

[209] Ibid., p 8

[210] Ibid., p 8

[211] Ibid., p 8

[212] Ibid., p 8

not advocating the other extreme of a purist Church which expects its members to already have reached perfection. He concludes that the institutionalisation he is speaking of is also true '*for a large part of the church*'[213] outside Germany.

The call for a '*divorce*'[214] by a retired pope is radical. In our time when quick fixes are culturally embedded in our psyche, such a radical call will necessitate patient and earnest resort to the Holy Spirit, and sincere communal fraternity.

Pope Francis wants us to listen in love to the difficult opinions of others; to believe that God is speaking truth through them also; to listen until it hurts, yet to listen in peace – Jesus has left us his own peace. His peace flows from the confidence that the Father is leading his people, and that when we love, even if it is scary, we will always be shown the direction through the Spirit. In calling his darling Church into the desert to speak to her heart, God thrills with the things he will teach her, and how beautiful she will become.

---

[213] Ibid., p 8
[214] Ibid., p 8

Two glimpses of the Church of the future

1. Querido Amazonia

In 2020 Pope Francis issued the Motu Proprio, *Querida Amazonia* (Beloved Amazonia)[215] summarising the outcomes of the Synod of the Amazon. The document expresses his love and dreams for that region of the world which is often described as its 'lungs'. He sees it as a microcosm of all the potential for change and renewal of our world and Church. Many commentators at the time expected him to pronounce on the question of married priests and the ordination of women, but he sees these issues as being worked out through the process of synodality which he is encouraging. The resolution of such issues would only be a minor alteration of the Church structure in response to people's urging today. What he focuses on is the far more important and central hope for reform which happens as all of us allow the Spirit to change us and lead us to take our part more fully in the whole process of re-creation which is the Church. The last section (from section 89 on) is the best and most encouraging outline of lay participation that I have read, and it is authoritative! It is worth reading thoughtfully.

---

[215] Francis Pope (2020) *Querida Amazonia* [online]. Rome. Holy See

2. Semillitas

When I visit a priest friend living in Marbella, Spain, I enjoy celebrating Mass with him in the parish where he worships. There the population is mostly Catholic, but very few come to Mass regularly. Like in Britain, the majority of people in Church are elderly, but more families attend on a regular basis. They have a large number of South Americans who have a different attachment to the faith, rather like the Poles, Asians and Africans in English parishes. In the Church in Spain generally the youth are absent.

Recently my friend urged me to watch a video of a Youth Mass in the parish. This showed about 100 children and youth at a Mass in their own Church which brought to an end a weekend away in a retreat centre. Various youngsters gave witnesses, and one boy spoke of how he had gone along to be with his mates but with little interest in religion. Then he went on to say that Jesus came to him on the Saturday night and now he was devoted to him. In the end he broke down and was surrounded by about 40 other youngsters who supported him and shielded him. These were assisted by their youth leaders, most of whom were young adults who practiced their faith, were well trained and had developed as a well organised team. I know that, in the future, the youngsters will meet many challenges to their faith and have doubts, but what a start!

I spoke to the parish priest, Father Rafa, and he told me that there had been years of gradually building up the youth outreach for it to reach this stage, and they used the **Semillitas**[216] programme, which I had never come across. It seems evident to me that this has a strong evangelising content as well as fun and games.

I know that the parishes in Spanish cities are usually much bigger than ours in the UK, but the number involved in that Youth Event and their depth of faith was exceptional. It was obvious that these youngsters operated in Christian peer groups. That seldom happens here even in our Catholic secondary schools, where there is often a strong anti-religious culture operating. It made me excited about what is possible when we cease to accept the way things are going, and listen deeply to the Holy Spirit. Father Rafa insisted that the major factors were prayer and recruiting the right people, among whom were pensioners. It does not surprise me that that parish has for a long time had 24 hour continual Exposition of the Blessed Sacrament.

---

[216] Semillitas de Emaus

Chapter 19

THE NEW EVANGELISATION

In 1990, Pope Saint John Paul II wrote: *'As the third millennium of the redemption draws near, God is preparing a great springtime for Christianity, and we can already see its first signs,'*[217] and he indicated that its first phase was what he called *'a New Evangelisation'*:

> *'In countries with ancient Christian roots, and occasionally in the younger Churches as well, entire groups of the baptised have lost a living sense of the faith, or even no longer consider themselves members of the Church, and live a life far removed from Christ and his Gospel. In this case what is needed is a **New Evangelisation or a re-evangelisation**'.*[218]

His successors, Benedict XIV and Francis have strongly reiterated his call for this *New Evangelisation*. Many people have been puzzled, because it has always

---

[217] John Paul II Pope St, (1990) *Redemptoris Missio* [online]. Rome. Holy See No. 33
[218] John Paul II Pope St, (1990) *Redemptoris Missio* [online]. Rome. Holy See No. 86

been the mission of the Church to evangelise. So, what is *New*? The simple answer is that this is aimed at Catholics, whereas previously evangelisation was aimed at non-believers. The concentration on Catholics in the *New Evangelisation* is a striking shift in emphasis on how the Church operates. It calls for some serious changes, and change is always hard. It calls for thoughtful prayer and a desire to do it well.

The Church evolving

Doing it well starts with us who are Church-going Catholics understanding the reason for this development. It is new because it is a fresh reemphasising of the original call of Jesus to his followers to be evangelised. That is to allow the Good News to set us on fire with the Spirit. Only then can we bring the Good News to others. The reason why we need *New Evangelisation* is because our traditional methods of ourselves being evangelised have broken down.

For centuries the Church has been busy developing a complicated system of operating in society, and we have become used to it. It is difficult to conceive that we need to change the model. We have to ask what has changed to make this model defective, and reflect seriously on what is the purpose of the model. It is also important to be very aware of what is working well in the old model and not endanger the good in striving for the perfect. Life evolves; it does not keep starting again from scratch. The faith of the Church has firm foundations, and is constantly altering its method of delivery as people and the world progress.

Society has changed

So what has changed to necessitate a New Evangelisation of Catholics? The answer is: Society has changed. In the second phase of her existence, the Church has sought to shape society according to Christian principles, and it has been largely effective, but it relied on a society which accepted authority easily or was effectively constrained to do so. Church communications were superb. The narrative that people interiorised was simple and the Church was good at shaping the narrative. It was largely taken for granted that society in the west was Christian. Within that sociological construct, many were enabled to grow in grace and holiness. Now that construct has been replaced.

The roll out of education, and the explosion of the media, along with a mounting stress on individual liberty have changed society. Simple acceptance of the way things are has been replaced by every person's right to work things out for themselves. The directing of society by accepted authorities and institutions has been downgraded, requiring them to prove their worth. This is a step forward in human development; it will not be reversed. The future belongs to either freedom or its opposite, despotism. Pope Benedict has warned that this culture change which has taken decades in the West will happen more rapidly in the developing world. No one can stop it.

Instead of dominating and directing society as in the past, the Church has to walk alongside human beings to help them use their freedom rightly. This developing freedom of people to choose for themselves grows out of humanity's dignity and likeness to God. It is a fruit of centuries of proclaiming the Gospel. Now that the fruit is maturing, the Church is needed more than ever to enable freedom to nourish humanity rather than cripple it. And to bring it into communion.

In the first flush of freedom's awakening on a large scale, individualism has grown, but society has become chaotic and community has become weaker. We are now at the point where the deep need for community is being felt. And yet there seem to be no real pointers to how it can flourish. But God has gifted his Church with communion, the divine power to bring about authentic community. We do not see the building of a good society as simply a human enterprise. We know that unity along with individuality is essentially Trinitarian. Humanity can only have both if they are in communion with God. The Church, the way God shares his blessed unity, has a wonderful role, indeed the central role, to play as humanity advances.

We are at the threshold of *a new normal*. It is nothing less than a third phase of the Church's journey. The Popes rightly point to the fact that the first requirement in this new age is for us Catholics to renew our attachment to our Father through Christ, and to be transformed by the awareness that we are redeemed. We can no longer expect society to teach us this. We have to be converted much more personally and carry society rather than be carried by it. Hence the need to know Christ more deeply and to be set on fire with the thirst to know him better, which sets us on a path of life-long prayer and learning. And, as we ourselves develop in faith and understanding, others will be drawn to the fire.

Not counter but catalyst

Some people make a lot of Christianity being a counter culture, but that is so narrow. We are the catalyst in the midst of the developing culture which helps it mature; we are the leaven in the dough. At times, we may seem to contradict, but that is because we have dreams of far greater development, not, as is often leveled at us, of narrow-mindedness. There will always be the tendency for people to take the easy bits of progress and ignore the hard work needed for true maturity. We have to be prepared to be misunderstood and attacked as we remind the world of the bigger picture. But progress always lies with those who take the pains to bring about full and proper growth.

An illustration

In this third phase of the Church, there will be the need to think outside the box, and be prepared to change the way we operate. Let me illustrate this from my own life experience. I appreciate that people elsewhere will have very different experiences, but all our experiences will coalesce because all the world is being led into the same reality of a new age. My priesthood has been in the north of England. For over thirty two of those years I have worked closely as a team with Anne Bardell who was the Pastoral Assistant in the parishes we served. Our joint reflections are contained in this book.

I would say that at least a third of our time was taken up with school work. In our area we have a whole system of Catholic schools. In the nineteenth century, as education itself developed, Catholics in our region put enormous efforts into building their own schools, because they suspected the ethos in state schools. Gradually, through political action, our Catholic school system has become mostly state funded, which has allowed for great development. Now In my time our schools are rightly reckoned among the best.

But society changed and so did Catholics. Originally, parents had, with great sacrifice, fiercely supported 'a Catholic education for every Catholic child' because they saw themselves defined by their faith. Gradually, that faith weakened under the influence of new ways of thinking, and now the Church identifies its schools as an outreach to Catholics and society at large. We still have many wonderful Catholic teachers, but fewer Catholic teachers are Church-goers and the lives of many give evidence of weak faith. Children generally come from homes where there is no prayer and which can only be described as nominally Catholic. Our education system is a laudable service given by the Church, but have we dedicated too much of our time and effort to this work concentrating on governance and running schools rather than evangelising?

We believe that we personally and others certainly have got the balance wrong. We worked for most of the time on the principle that putting great effort into governorship and helping the schools to be at the forefront of educational progress would give us a platform for influencing the schools to deepen their spiritual mission, but, despite the hard work, things only marginally improved. Educational change was moving too fast and strongly in the opposite direction. I can hear St Paul challenging us and those who, like us, have relied on our school system to evanglise in the same words which he wrote to the Corinthians who were celebrating the Eucharist in an unbalanced way: '*Do I praise you? In this I praise you not.*'[219]

Looking at this more deeply: Parents are judging our schools, often superficially, by the marks they receive from government inspectors, which causes schools to make feverish efforts to achieve top grades. This leads to teacher selection based on evidence of skills in imparting the curriculum and their effectiveness academically. This makes some practicing Catholic teachers seem second best. Their witness of faith and the ability to engender a Catholic ethos can be downplayed. If that becomes the norm then our schools will be little different to state schools. Surely, if that happens, it will be the time to become more radical in our teacher selection procedures or to give the schools to the State. The time and money our parishes spend on our schools might then be better spent on evangelising and catechising adults. Possibly, both forms of education, schools and adult catechetics, can be achieved together, but the enormous effort put into the former compared to the dearth of investment in the latter is putting the cart before the horse. We will never improve our schools as authentic witnesses to life in

---

[219] 1 Cor 1: 22

Christ, if we do not improve our ways of leading adults into greater faith and conviction.

Enormous effort is put into leading children to First Communion. Most children along with their parents have no real connection with Church. At this time it is adult Catholics who need evangelising. Only parents who know and live their faith will be able, as the first teachers of their children, to effectively lead them on the path of faith. When the first teaching in the home is not in place, the second teaching in school has proved to be ineffective. So much of children's sacramental preparation in parishes is aimed at the child with parents being sidelined. Without a renewal of parental faith, it is no wonder that the effects of our programmes are so meager. Changing our way of working calls for serious thought. It will be gradual and involve many small steps, but we must change.

We are putting the wine of a new age into old wineskins. Better to craft new wineskins. God so much wants to get through his Church to the people he yearns for. We express these views as people who have worked as hard as anyone to implement the school system and sacramental programmes as we received them. That entitles us to be taken seriously when we evaluate the system.

Chapter 20

FORWARD

Here, the word 'forward' does not denote the section at the beginning of a book, but the direction in which Jesus is leading his Church. Luke[220] tells us that, after the previous day's spectacular success of Jesus' ministry in Capernaum, the disciples urge him to go back. He, however, has spent long hours in a lonely place seeking his Father's direction while they had been sleeping. He tells them that there is a far greater outreach before them. Instead of consolidating what they think they have achieved so far, they are to see it as the beginning of a journey. The Father will lead him and his close followers, in ways that will not always seem clear, to a point that will seem at first like utter failure, but will be final success. Success because, in him, faithful humanity calls down the overflow of heaven to earth. That moment itself will be the beginning of a journey for his people, which we have each joined in our own time.

It is a journey of struggle shot through with moments of wonderful enlightenment. Church documents call the members of this movement God's *'faithful*

---

[220] Lk 4: 42-44

people'.[221] That is not a description of people who never have doubts, but of those who struggle through unknowingly towards the knowing that comes from God. They do this because they put their trust in Jesus. Faith is the act of the will by which we open up a landing strip for the activity of God to come down. Hope is the utter conviction that God's loving plan is working even in hard times. Faith, hope and Agape are gift which the Lord fixes into the hearts of his faithful.

Taking out of the treasure house things both new and old

In these writings we have tried to share the wonderful vision we have of the Church as she is being prepared for the third phase of her journey. We do not speak from bitterness and disappointment, but from a conviction that the storms we are all living through have a purpose in God's plan. His plan is as glorious and amazing as it has ever been. The new age that is dawning is in his hands. If we have seemed negative in anything we have written, that is not our intention, neither are we calling for a wholesale revolution. The Church like her master is prudent *'taking from the treasure store things that are old and new'*.[222] Let me give an example of how God renews the ancient treasures the Church has been graced with.

---

[221] Holy See, *Catechism of the Catholic Church,* London Geoffrey Chapman, A Cassell imprint 1945 para 897 ff
[222] Mt 13: 52

Loreto

People in Western Europe have believed for centuries that the little house of Loreto, Italy, was the real house in which the Holy Family lived in Nazareth. They accepted the tale that it had been transported by angels to that special place. Now in our rational age, many do not believe that. Does that mean that all those pilgrims from past ages were deluded? No. The story they took to be true may have been a notional untruth, but, for most, the experience they had as they imagined themselves in the holy house was of deep prayer and inspiration.

Imagination is essential in prayer, and places like Loreto feed the imagination and produced deep prayer. People's awareness opened to understanding how the Holy Family worked and that encouraged their own family life. They imagined St Joseph teaching Jesus at the workbench and saw themselves there. They pictured Mary cooking and washing and realised the holiness of their own humdrum human work. They came away more united to God. They could not go to Nazareth, but they could feel Nazareth. Holy places are privileged venues that lift people's minds and hearts to God. Maybe we can go to Israel more easily today, but that was how folk in past ages went there virtually. And it still works today. Even if you doubt the truth of the legend, people still come profoundly close to the Holy Family there and feel their own family life strengthened. The ease with which people overlook the improbability of the story of Loreto is a witness to the hunger we have to touch and feel the Divine. We need aids to prayer. Added to that, countless people experience the sense of holiness that is normal in shrines which have been the focus of prayer for centuries.

It would be folly to label instances like this as superstition and dismiss them. Superstition is where we embrace untruth in order to imagine that we have some special power over reality; something that builds our feeling of self-sufficiency. Faith is where we step out of our self-sufficiency and open up to God. It would only be superstition if God did not exist. So far those rationalists, who demand convincing proofs for everything, have been unable to offer proof that there is no God. The overwhelming volume of human experience indicates God's existence and the rationale of faith.

The stream that floods

In the last few years before the Babylonians destroyed Judea and Jerusalem, the prophet Ezekiel had to publish vivid visions of stark and damning warning to the Jews. Endemic corruption and wholesale desertion of God had reached so terrible a state, and they had ignored the warning of the prophets so much that calamitous consequences were unavoidable. The first part of his book echoes with dire predictions. Yet within it all, God's anger is characterised as the reaction of a spurned lover. When Ezekiel beholds the Glory of the Lord finally leaving the temple because he is unwanted, the Lord hovers almost reluctantly as one who is loath to go and leave them to the terrible destruction they have called down upon themselves.[223]

---

[223] Ez 11: 22-23

The second part of his book, written after the Babylonian war, changes to prophecies of how, after the loss of everything they owned, and the slaughter of the majority of their nation, the remnant, who had been transported to Babylon as slaves, would return to the Promised Land, and their relationship with God would revive.

This revival was partially achieved by the time Christ was born; the Jews of Jesus' time generally led a genuine religious life. But it was only after Christ opened the gates of heaven from the cross that some of Ezekiel's prophecies were truly fulfilled, as when he had prophesied that the Spirit would be poured out and we would be given new hearts of flesh to replace our hearts of stone.[224]

In the last of his vivid visions,[225] Ezekiel sees a stream flowing from the right hand side of the Temple, which grows into a mighty river of healing and life-giving water. Its banks would burst forth with fruit and the waters of the river would cause the seas to team with abundant life. This was a direct reference to the fact that, after Christ had breathed his life into the Father's hands, his heart was pierced by the soldier's lance, and in blood and water the Holy Spirit gushed forth. That outpouring is the Church, the promised flooding into our world of the Spirit to recreate and renew the face of the earth.

---

[224] Ez 11: 18-19
[225] Ez 47: 1-12

Today, we agonise and squabble about sharing the fruits of the earth, and vividly see how human cast-offs are tainting the oceans. God gave the prophet a vision and promise of wholeness and abundance, but it comes as the river of the Spirit flows and swells. An intriguing detail of the vision speaks of how the river at first comes only to the ankles, but then to the waist, and then becomes so deep that a person cannot wade across, but only be carried along in the flow. That could be a picture of how the Church has grown through different phases.

When the stream was so low that it came only to ankles, it was the age when mankind tried to ignore it and tramp it out. When it was waist high, people struggled to embrace the Spirit, but many attempted to accommodate it to their own pedestrian ways. In the third phase of the Church which is now dawning, the only way is to abandon ourselves to the grace and flow of the Spirit, and penetrate the whole world with the reality of Christ.

Multiple golden threads

The story of the Church is one of gradual development, outside of human planning, following the paths that God gradually unwinds before us like rolling balls of golden thread. The paths are marked by frequent crosses, but also growing light. In the third age of the Church, Christ's faithful people, men and women who increasingly exercise their Royal Priesthood in every corner of the world, are the key to human development and 'renewing the face of the earth'.[226] This is not replacing the coming of the Kingdom which we pray for in the second part of the Lord's prayer, but complementing it with the third part, '*Thy will be done on earth as it is in heaven*'.[227]

I believe this time we have been living through has been especially pivotal in the process of salvation. One clear sign of this is that, during our time, God has sent us popes of extraordinary stature to guide us through the turmoil of transition. Each has endured great hardship before their election, often at the hands of fellow Catholics, and each was aware of their own limitations, but over the decades, in the seemingly crazy crises and calamities, the path forward has been enlightened by their onward journeys of faith. As I look back, I can see clear signs such as this that God is moving his people forward to fulfil his purpose.

Views of how this will be achieved vary. Some say that the world will carry on in its own mad ways and that the people of God will live through it until the Lord arrives in judgment, and then many who have followed the world will be damned. They interpret the above passage of Ezekiel as only having spiritual meaning and not a prophecy of our world maturing under the Spirit's leading. I personally cannot reconcile this with the God who has gradually, but more and more clearly, revealed his unlimited and urgent love for all mankind. While ignorant of God's timing, I still

---

[226] Ps 104: 30
[227] Mt 6:10

perceive the journey of God's people as one of gradually renewing the earth, increasingly becoming effective in baptising the nations in the name of the Father and of the Son and of the Holy Spirit.[228] Teaching them to observe the commandments of love

Because of the generous and infinite love of God, the Spirit is '*at play everywhere in his world, delighting to be with the children of men'*.[229] Each of us, as we seek the face of God, will find our destined path made clear before us. The Father and Son will be at home with us.[230] The unity of the indwelling Trinity will draw us to one another in the Church. Christ wishes, through the members of his mystical body, to draw the world to wholeness. The '*enterprise is begun; it is of God; it cannot be withstood'*.[231]

The deep fact of which our Christian faith assures us of is that God is mysteriously but surely calling all humanity into the Trinity, his family. God's methods may seem obscure to minds that demand certainty, but they reveal themselves to his lovers who follow him humbly through this beautiful but perplexing world.

The most beautiful, holy, loving Spirit of God will never leave us. We are like the disciples after the

---

228 Mt 28: 18-20

229 Prv 8: 31

230 Jn 14: 23

231 E. Campion St, (1781) *Challenge to the Privy Council (Campion's "Brag")*[online] Catholic answers 1994 Catholic cutlure.org No. 8

Ascension of Jesus who were told to wait in Jerusalem for the gift of the Holy Spirit. We, like them, pray that, in his great and tender mercy, he will descend afresh on all humanity for his sweet names sake. Amen.

SECTION IV

PRACTICAL CONSIDERATIONS FOR PARISH ADULT CATECHETICS

Introduction to this Section

All the previous chapters have been written by myself, Fr Brian Murphy, with the constant help, revision and collaboration of Anne Bardell who worked with me for 32 years in two parishes as Pastoral Assistant. My writing is from the point of view of a pastor and preacher. Anne's is from the point of view of a practitioner of teaching the faith at all levels. She has widely studied schemes and programmes from around the world, and led the implementation of some of them in the parishes in which we worked. She has special experience and competence as a catechist with a Licentiate in Catechetics. In these chapters, she writes about putting into practise some innovative ideas to enable adults to grow deeply in their faith in a variety of ways.

Chapter 21

THE SITUATION IN MANY OF OUR PARISHES TODAY

Our aim was to light the fire within adults to know their faith

Throughout the 32 years that I worked in a team partnership with Fr. Brian, our main aim was to help practising adults know their faith, and to reintroduce parents, with little Church contact back into the faith. We always considered the parents to be the most important builders of Church and the older generations as the powerhouse of prayer. We tried many different ways to reach folk, always asking the question 'will this help them to grow more deeply in their faith?' We put on a variety of courses in the parish – day retreats, evenings, weekends, Lent and Advent programmes just like in many other parishes. But taking a step further, we explored many different materials[232] and were adventurous and innovative, using and creating new methods and material, with our focus always centred on where we believed the Holy Spirit was leading. If something failed we would then try a different approach

---

[232] For example 'Echoes' from Maryvale Institute, ' Discovering Christ' from Christlife.org

and if we could not find the material we needed, we created it.

During our years in parish work we sought to create an ethos of welcome and care for everyone in the parish family. People really loved this family atmosphere which caused a chain reaction as they began to welcome others. Within this family who were growing in faith together, we tried to connect people to Scripture, Tradition and Magisterium as well as to the developing, living Catholic Church.

In these last four chapters I will try to share some of the things that bothered us and some of the attempts we made to develop new strategies. Reaching out to educate parents as catechists of their children was a central part of our work alongside our main goal of assisting the laity to become educated in the faith and understand their Christian heritage. The intention was that an informed laity could then be trained to assist in passing on the faith, which would be essential if our parishes are to be developed as hubs of adult faith learning. I have also written here about the personal search of every Catholic to gain a greater understanding of the faith. The centre of this idea is not just about a body of knowledge but about knowing how to develop and deepen a personal relationship with Jesus.

Finally there is a mention of Synodality which is the hot topic in our Church at this moment, but it is something that should be part of our Church's decision making processes in the future. It essentially means we need to listen to the Holy Spirit speaking through laity and clerics alike, speaking through a Church which needs to move forward in unison according to God's plan.

Today's society based on lack of trust

The majority of practising Catholics want the Church to respond immediately to everything that happens in the world and have little understanding that the Church exists within the arc of history, and therefore, things take a long time to develop and grow. The arc of history stretches across vast amounts of time and our life span is a minute proportion of it. Hurts caused by persecution from outside or the sins of a few within the Church can take many years to be healed. The same can be said about the development of new pathways created over many years which speak to and attract people to the Lord and his Church in an ever changing world. The Church is a living entity, always changing and growing, but it does not happen overnight and it only changes according to God's plan.

When we look at today's society in comparison with fifty years ago, it has radically changed. People were raised in a society where there was respect for institutions and trust in authority and in the Church. Over the decades that has been whittled away, so much so that people are not sure who to trust. The evil one has been busy, for example the child sex abuse scandal in the Church has not only permanently damaged the victims, it permanently damaged the view of the Church in the eyes of its many members. Individuals within worshipping communities had put their trust in these 'holy people' of God and the sad thing is, that many good people and good leaders of the Church were tainted and suffered as a result of the backlash against those few who were acting with evil intentions.

Once that layer of trust in Church authority and guidance was eroded, something was needed to fill the gap, and that was based on what people knew well and trusted, that is themselves. Increasingly people have become authorities on everything, using the internet to provide their answers. They began to believe that they could assert their right to everything they desired, and that no-one has the right to tell them how to think or behave, including the Church authorities. They stopped listening to the Church and as a result stopped understanding the very essence of our faith, our rituals and the graces bestowed.

Church rituals unknown by many

This means that we have parents and grandparents who have become disconnected from the Church, and they have little idea of Church guidance, or the depth of faith that previous generations had.

Recently I watched the Blessed Sacrament carried around the Underground Basilica in Lourdes. The Basilica holds thousands but was almost empty (which is a statement in itself), and out of the hundred or so people present, many seemed to be lacking in the knowledge of how to behave when the Blessed Sacrament was brought near to them for each to be blessed by our Sovereign Lord. In the past there would have been great reverence and respect, and for some that was still present, but others did not know whether to stand, sit or kneel and only made the sign of the cross when they saw others doing it. I am sure they meant no disrespect but they seemed to have no knowledge of how to bow or kneel in humility in the Lord's presence. This is just one example providing evidence that we have several generations who were not embedded in the rituals or knowledge of the faith.

Many have a rudimentary knowledge of the faith

Further evidence of this disconnection from the Church and from daily practise of our faith, and its value, is shown in the story referred to elsewhere in this book. It is the story about a young mum on our Sacramental Programme who came early to Mass on Palm Sunday, as we requested, in order to make palm leaves with their child to use in the joy filled entrance procession. Her deliberate action of waiting until I was near to her to start proclaiming loudly about how ridiculous it was to be asked to come to Mass (during Holy Week) in the school holidays as well as at a weekend, showed the lack of understanding she had of Holy Week or even of the importance of the Eucharist. Her comment about 'do these people not think we have a life outside of Church stuff?' was very telling about where the practise of the faith fitted into her life style.

We began to wonder what on earth these parents were doing attending the Sacramental Programme and what needed to change. We realised that when others teach their children about the faith, whether it be the school or catechists, parents take a back seat through lack of confidence in faith matters and a feeling that it is not their responsibility. The simple act of appointing a catechist to teach a child about the faith signals in neon lights to the parents that they are not capable, not sufficiently committed, or perhaps do not have the skills or faith knowledge to teach their own child about the faith. A prime example of this was voiced by one of our parents who regularly attended Church, when he said 'I would not know where to start. I don't know enough about my faith to teach my girls as I would surely miss out important things, so I will leave it to the experts'. Therefore the responsibility is pushed onto schools and the Church whilst parents sit in the background and are unable to fulfil the promise they made at Baptism to raise their child in the faith; they leave that to others.

Faith seekers and rediscoverers need immersion in a learning faith community

Some who come asking for Baptism for their children have had only glimpses of the incredible gift of faith and they want to understand and know everything from the beginning and want it for their child. They are eager and thirsty for opportunities to pursue their quest in knowing more about God. Others want Baptism because 'we are Catholics and that is what we do in our family' or 'my Mum or grandma thinks it is the right thing to do', yet they rarely, if ever, attend Mass. In Britain some people want their child Baptised to ensure they have a place in the local Catholic school.[233] For others it is a process of rediscovering the faith that they have lost all real connection with, yet without any help or support we expect them to come to Mass, which is like an alien language to them, and they are expected to be instantly part of the community when they know no-one.

It is evident, therefore, that there needs to be a very gentle programme of immersion and welcome into the worshipping faith community for these parents. The parish should be a community where learning about your faith is the norm, whilst allowing everyone to learn at their own pace, and enable everyone to take their rightful place in the worshipping community. This would mean that there should be a continual faith-learning train travelling on set tracks within a parish for any parishioner to step on and off as work and events in life permit. If the atmosphere in a parish is that adults continue to learn about their faith in order to deepen their relationship with Jesus, then young adults would be absorbed into this system of a learning community after the baptism of their children. When the time arrives for preparation for other Sacraments of Initiation, parents who have accessed this faith-learning train after Baptism preparation, would then already be embedded in the practise of the faith, which would receive a further boost during the Sacramental Programme.

---

[233] In England and Wales the Government covers that majority of the cost of Catholic schools and the admission criteria gives priority to Cahtolic Baptised children.

If we can train catechists to work with children and hold parents' meetings, why can we not train catechists to catechise parents to enable them to catechise their own children? We did this in our parishes and it relit many parents' faith and enabled them to carry out the responsibility they accepted at Baptism to pass on the faith to their child with confidence. A further question arises about whether these, or similar catechists, could also hold evenings / daytime events on the faith train in their parish for the ordinary practising Catholics to discuss their faith at a deeper level, but we will return to this later.

Chapter 22

THINKING OUTSIDE THE BOX ABOUT PARISH PROGRAMMES

The Church processes need renovation

When people come and ask for Baptism for their child, many turn up for a couple of sessions, attend the Baptismal ceremony and disappear. How is that acceptable as joining the Church? They reappear six or seven years later to get ready for the celebration of First Communion, often giving scant time to the preparation they need to do with their child, due to work and other commitments. Then we will not see most of them again apart from in our Catholic schools or when there is an event such as a family funeral. Obviously not everyone is like this, but this trend has grown over the years. Therefore we need to accept that the Church processes are not working, and are in great need of renovation, not just the Church buildings and parish boundaries.

This renovation of adult evangelisation needs to be rolled out wholesale in a country or even a diocese. There should also be an expectation expressed by the Church that 'this is what we do as Catholics' to ensure faith learning becomes the norm in parishes. Otherwise faithful parishioners will not think it applies to them and parents will play one parish off against another with the common chat at the school gates being 'I will go to St. Elsewhere's for the Sacramental Programme, as you have to do a lot less work'. We all know this happens and just seem to accept this is the status quo.

Of those who faithfully practise within a worshipping community, many have a rudimentary knowledge of the history and/or development of the faith, or the Church. Many of our older worshippers have faith based on instruction given at school before the time of the Second Vatican Council (1962-1964) or around that time, when we really did not understand its message for the Church. We know this is the case, but instead of encouraging them to seek a greater understanding of their faith, we are just happy that they keep practising and add their number to the congregations.

We are at the point in our Church where we must ask ourselves 'are we doing the Holy Spirit a disservice by not listening and following his lead as he tries to rock us out of this rut where we seem stuck?' The rut is the conviction that 'I know enough about my faith' without any thought about what more there is to learn. We need to ask what other riches are there to discover in the faith and what is the Holy Spirit saying to us that we do not hear?

Thinking outside the box and beyond

Recently I studied some current Sacramental Programmes and was dismayed to find that in the majority, parish catechists are still taking over the role of catechising the children, with parents walking along side ensuring they fill in their workbook. We tried this approach thirty years ago and are saddened to find that recent online information indicates that the majority of diocesan/ parish catechetical programmes still follow this path. This only engages with parents in a friendly way, but not really a faith sharing way. It is important to recognise that if a child is to be raised in the faith, it should be the parents who are nurtured, to enable them to catechise their child.

We know it is not an easy task to establish such a programme. For several years we tried to help the parents to be the catechists of their children by creating child friendly workbooks for the children to complete whilst, at the same time, giving the parents an identical book with the answers. This meant they could catechise their child and know what they were teaching was correct, which gave them confidence and helped parents to rediscover their faith at the same time. To help to prepare them for this role, we held eight parents' meetings in the year (one for each module) and discussed one aspect of the faith, for example Reconciliation, to help them first to understand it at an adult level, and then we walked them through the workbooks which they then took home to complete with their child. This was partially successful, but as the years progressed, parents were displaying more and more basic unfamiliarity with the Church and simple family practice of the faith. Simple things stood out such as parents not knowing who the statues represented in Church, how to genuflect or even know what the tabernacle is for.

After the experience of the comments on Palm Sunday previously described, we decided to think further outside the box and we began to understand that the parents needed a renewal of their faith before they could share it. We began to look around for new programmes to help us to reach out to these adults, but we found very little of value. Then we discovered '*Divine Renovation*'[234] through which Fr. James Mallon inspired us to think along new tracks to enable Catholics to deepen their faith.

We decided to change tack and gathered a group of concerned Catholics from the parish. These parishioners were led to delve together into the riches of their faith through training within the parish. They became well-formed in the faith and eager to know more. This gave them the confidence in the faith and they wanted to share this with others. When we suggested they help with parent groups they were at first hesitant but also eager to assist in the process of reaching out to parents. So with great trepidation we took the next step.

Our next step was to begin to invite Sacramental programme parents to adult sessions with this group of parishioners who were well formed in the faith (although they were trembling in their shoes). We also invited others from the parish to join these discussion groups to relook at their faith.

During evenings with a time of prayer, a shared meal and discussion led groups, the parents began to

---

[234] Fr J. Mallon (2016) *Divine Renovation* (Toronto: Novalis 2016)

blossom. They were ecstatic about the idea of sharing with other adults about what they did or didn't know about the faith without being judged, and were gently led so that they felt comfortable to ask questions without embarrassment. One thing that surprised us, was how they also appreciated a hot meal which they had not cooked, and time with other adults talking about faith, which they seldom had experienced. These were the first steps in making them feel accepted and enabled them to refresh their knowledge and understanding of the faith with a view to passing it on to others, primarily their children.

Once the parents came to know others in the parish during these discussion nights we encouraged them to join the worshipping community. The parishioners, knowing the trepidation of the parents, then went out of their way to welcome them at a Sunday Mass and often sat with them or near them. This helped the parents to feel more comfortable during the liturgy and they were automatically invited by the parishioners to join the tea/coffee after Mass and to come to other parish events such as the Christmas Fair and the Blessed Sacrament Procession. In other words they were welcomed into the community without any kind of pressure.

Raising children in the faith

We know that young children ask many questions about everything, including the faith, and often parents are at a loss to answer when they have a limited knowledge of the Church and Catholic teachings. This role only becomes more difficult as the children become older when the onus is on the parent or other adults to raise the topic of our belief and life in Jesus with teenagers and young adults in the family.

After talking with many parents who have grown up children with families of their own, their constant cry was of the wound they felt when they thought they had done everything possible to raise their children in the faith. Their children had turned out to be the best people with great families, but faith had little or no relevance in their lives. This has left the parents asking "What did we do wrong?"

Perhaps there is another element present here, which is that the Church is slow to help parents to adapt the way they handed on the faith in a rapidly changing culture. An example of a recent change is the manipulation of younger adults through online influencers, adverts and media which promotes the dream that the 'good life' is attainable. Unless we take on the responsibility of helping people acquire the necessary skills to deal with these seemingly insurmountable situations, they are left with a feeling of powerlessness which becomes concrete. Conversations about a relationship with Jesus are circumvented and the topic becomes the snoozing elephant in the room which is easier to avoid than to raise to its feet.

When you read in *Christifideles Laici*[235] that the role of the laity, bestowed at Baptism, is to spread the

---

[235] John Paul II Pope St, (1988) *Christifideles Laici* [online]. Rome. Holy See para 15: 29, 37, 41

word of God in their families, homes and places of work, one has to ask, 'what is it that folk will be spreading?' If they do not know their faith or how, in this present ever changing culture, to live according to Jesus' teachings, how can they share it with others? Ask any Catholic how they would talk to someone who does not know Jesus, or believes but does not practise the faith, and the majority would say 'I have no idea; that is the job of the priest, the Church or the school'. This emphasises the need for adult education in the faith if we are to enable folk to carry out our baptismal responsibility of spreading the Good News.

Chapter 23

DEVELOPING PARISHES AS PLACES OF ADULT FAITH LEARNING

How welcoming are our Parishes?

Before we look at how to begin to think about solving the issue of adult faith education we need to consider another difficulty that is thrown into the mix in our parishes. 'How welcoming is our parish?' This is a question we need to be constantly asking our congregations. Let me open up this package a little further. After standing at the door of the Church at every weekend Mass for over 30 years, I have watched people come and go, listened to and had the privilege of sharing in all sorts of problems, sadnesses and joys with folk. However, I have also seen faithful parishioners, good people who practise week-in and week-out, only talk to those they know. Young families or new parishioners would often arrive nervously and make their way inside Church, but, once there, no-one came near them except for a cursory glance or worse still to interrogate them. Our parish communities need to change. They are not meant to only belong to those who have attended since the dark ages and have developed into well-formed cliques, or, worse still, to be power bases for some people's little empires.

Parishes are meant to be communities based on Jesus, they are for everyone and should be open and accepting places with a warm and genuine welcome. Sadly many of our parish communities have become a group of small cliques and new people can often feel on the outside. On one of the Scottish islands they call new people '*incomers*' and you only lose this status and become accepted after 50 or 60 years residing there. The word '*incomer*' often reminds me of the atmosphere in many of the parishes that I have visited when not working. I think we have much to learn from the welcoming atmosphere of the new Evangelical Churches which are growing fast amongst the young as they provide a welcoming inclusive family atmosphere. On the rare occasions when newcomers are welcomed into an inclusive Catholic Parish and they come to discuss their faith at an adult level, then they stay and seek more connections and become valued members of the worshipping community.

Therefore, we have to ask the question today in parishes of 'how welcoming is your parish?' I bet half the people reading this will say 'we love to welcome new folk' but is this followed up by someone physically making a sustained effort to speak to newcomers, to invite them to events, to phone and just say 'hello', or meet up for coffee without them feeling they are being given the third degree of interrogation? Probably the answer is 'No'. I always remember a story told by my old mum who had been attending a Church (not her own parish) that she could reach by bus on a Sunday, when she became unable to walk far. After attending each week and sometimes during the week for about five years, she decided she would like to join a pilgrimage to Pantasaph. She was abruptly told by the person taking the names 'you are not part of our parish, so you cannot come'. Quite a Christian response!

On another occasion I remember a man who had become a Catholic after going through our RCIA programme and then had fallen away from weekly Mass. He nervously turned up one Sunday morning and I was so pleased to see him, only to discover there had been real problems in the family which had prevented him attending. Just as we were chatting and he was beginning to settle, along came a parishioner who, in a very loud voice declared 'Crikey, it's a long time since we have seen you, what are you doing here?' The guy was mortified. Sadly, to my knowledge, he never returned to Church.

So yes, our parishes definitely have to change to become more Christ-like. Skills of welcoming need developing, for example, a simple offer to a newcomer of 'you are welcome to come and sit with me, and then at least you will know one person in the parish' could help them feel at home. On a recent trip to Spain when attending the local parish Church I was welcomed and invited to have a coffee with someone, even though I was only there for a few days – this was a really welcoming gesture. Another simple thing that we tried in our parishes at the beginning of Mass, was to invite and encourage people to introduce themselves to those around them. It is amazing how people need to be introduced before they start to form a relationship; they can sit near someone each week for years but never know their name or anything about them.

Start with a level playing field

We also need to be aware that people are very nervous about coming to anything at Church when they have been away from it for a while or have never attended. Even for those who attend regularly, their anxiety sky rockets if they think they will need to declare they don't know something about their faith and feel they will be judged for it. This means it is essential with any adult faith course that it starts with a level playing field, which means no question or discussion is too silly or looked down on. For some reason within the Church in this country there is an atmosphere of 'well, I should know that about my faith' so it becomes difficult to admit that there are things that I have forgotten or never learnt. A relaxed informal atmosphere gently helps people to say 'what about this?' and 'what does the Church say about that?'

Adult Faith journeys

During the past generations many learnt about their faith through constant immersion in a family who practised the faith, through the Sacrament of Reconciliation and weekly Mass, together with prayer and faith discussions in the home or with friends. This scenario of being raised in the faith has all but disappeared and so we need to investigate how the Church can fill this gap through adult faith education.

Adult faith journeys develop along different paths and for many their faith developed after contact with people who are deeply embedded faithful Catholics who witness to their faith through the lives they lead, the words they speak, their morals and the actions they take. When people are seeking a greater depth of faith they are often introduced to the many dimensions of our belief through an RCIA course which is usually well catered for in parishes. However, once that is completed there is nothing for these new Catholics to click into or join to continue their faith search journey.

Over the years of working with adults it has become crystal clear that many Catholics learn far more from input combined with directed and informal discussions than any other method of learning, yet these are rarely provided for in our busy parishes. It's not rocket science; it's common sense that we need to know and share our heritage and to encourage the development of a thirst to learn more. But as our parishes get bigger with less clergy, anything other than traditional ministries tends to be put on the back burner. They are simply reacting to immediate demands, rather than being proactive, and planning for the future is side-lined. This means that adult faith education may never re-emerge even though it is essential for the future growth of the Church.

What does a course for adults need to include?

When we look into the present scene where diocese or parishes make an attempt at providing extra events to enrich the faith practise of congregants, we often find a pattern of attendees being talked 'at' rather than 'shared with'. At the majority of Church events where a speaker is invited, they often give their presentation, followed by a few moments of questions, if time allows. It is very rare that there is a chance for discussion and feedback, allowing a conversation on the subject, and yet most adults learn through an input/ discussion type scenario. It is clear that there are very few occasions when adults have the opportunity to discuss their faith within the life of a parish.

It isn't just a matter of not having the opportunity. Sherry Weddell[236] (a great analyst of Catholic attitudes) highlights the fact that Catholics seem to avoid talking about Jesus and their faith. They are great at talking about anything else, but not this. She calls it the 'culture of silence'.[237]

Many people may be great at coming to weekly or even daily Mass but have never looked much beyond this. However, we discovered over the years of working in parishes that people come alive when they learn about and understand the background and foundations that underpin their faith. This type of learning seems to be most effective in informal sessions where discussion is an essential part of the evening.

[236] S A. Weddell *Forming Intentional Disciples: The Path to Knowing and Following Jesus* (Huntington: Our Sunday Visitor Publications Division, 2012) pp. 56
[237] S A. Weddell *Forming Intentional Disciples: The Path to Knowing and Following Jesus* (Huntington: Our Sunday Visitor Publications Division, 2012) pp. 189-190

One off-shoot of these faith discussions is that attendees gain confidence in their faith knowledge and they often realise they know more than they thought they did. All of this increases their confidence in raising faith topics in discussions with friends and family and it is no longer a taboo subject.

Provision of opportunities to discuss our faith

Parishes need to provide these opportunities for people to increase their knowledge and understanding of the faith. Informal group chats could cover elements such as something of the history of the development of the Church from the beginning, a knowledge of the Real Presence of Jesus in the Eucharist, how to develop a relationship with Jesus, an understanding of the Trinity, Mary and the saints, and a knowledge of scripture and its context. Other topics for group discussion could be taken from suggestions from the attendees. We found that people always raised questions about Church teaching on annulments, separation, divorce and marriage and questions of all types on morals.

One example of adults enjoying learning about their faith came when completing the online Bible History Timeline course[238] with a friend, who was deeply ingrained in the faith. This course included times of sharing thoughts about a particular event on the timeline and how it spoke to us in our daily life. This sharing via phone conversations and Zoom during Covid lockdown opened both our eyes to see things

---

[238] M &J. Iannicelli Bible Timeline Course [online]

from another viewpoint, as a new light shone on different facets of the history of the faith. She came alive with things she had never known before or had only seen glimpses of, but now they had fallen into their rightful place in her bank of knowledge.

Gradual nurturing

There is so much that could be included in these discussion nights but we cannot throw the whole book at folks, it needs to be a gentle start. Once people have become fascinated with investigating and sharing their faith, it will lead them to new depths of faith learning which could be done in frequently repeated modules to allow anyone to click into them in their own time. The faith-learning or discovery train moving on a cyclical track in a parish would allow people to hop on and off, and access faith modules as family life and work permits. Initially caution should be taken to ensure that fundamentals of the faith are acquired in a systematic way to prevent learning becoming 'pick and mix'.

The place of prayer in faith learning

One of the most important elements of any course / programme however is prayer, as without this we are simply going through a mechanical exercise of discovery using our brain not our heart. When prayer is central in any learning situation, God guides our faith discovery and it enriches the very core of our faith and directs our heart in our practise of the faith. So every learning situation needs to be wrapped in prayer, so that it becomes as familiar as breathing.

The skill of trained leaders

After some form of input, perhaps through a short video clip on a particular topic or a short talk, there needs to be well-led discussions with well-trained good listening leaders. The input and questions could be delivered by Zoom for those unable to physically attend on certain occasions. The whole range of media could be used to ensure it is presented in modern ways so as to attract the young. But the most important part of the whole process is the skill of trained lay leaders as they listen and facilitate the discussion in the groups whether it be in person or by zoom.

What material is available for adult faith discussion courses?

When we take a look at what is available for adults to learn about the faith at a greater depth within parishes, there is little on offer, with one or two exceptions such as programmes by Bishop Barron '*Word on Fire*'[239] series or *Sycamore* by Fr. Stephen Wang[240] which could be easily used to begin the faith conversations.

A good example of modular learning is developing at the Franciscan University of Steubenville in Ohio.

---

[239] Bishop Barron *Word on Fire Series: Proclaiming Christ in the Culture* [online]

[240] Fr S. Wang (2021) *Sycamore: The Catholic Faith Explained* [online]

They are creating a system of online learning in their Catechetical Institute[241] under Dr. Petroc Willey and Dr. Bill Keimig. This is mainly aimed at Catechists and leaders, diocese, parishes and large groups but individuals can also buy into this system. It consists of 10- 20 minute video clips followed by online questions to discuss, ponder and study at their own pace at home, and recently Steubenville have added online discussion groups led by a mentor. The number of workshops is growing all the time and many are now available in Spanish as well as English. An added facility is provided for a diocese, group or a parish to specify a combination of workshops in a unique list that they wish their members to have access to for a particular project e.g. youth leaders. This would provide the input which could be followed up through discussion with a local mentor via Zoom or in person. This would allow groups to watch the clips together and discus or for indiviuals in these groups to study a module in their own time and then gather with the group to discuss it.

The lack of adult faith discussion projects

However, further research shows that the field of good systematic adult faith discussion programmes to promote adult faith learning is inadequate and often none existent in parishes generally. Many who are seeking a greater depth of faith and a chance to discuss

---

[241] Franciscan University of Steubenville Catechetical Institute – called 'Franciscan at home' [online] available at https://franciscanathome.com

their faith are often invited to attend existing RCIA[242] programmes which are really designed for those outside the faith who are seeking answers to basic questions. Generally, other available pathways for research into the faith follow an academic route leading to a degree or some other qualification in Theology, which is not the appropriate or desired route for most people.

Learning about the core of our faith

As previously discussed the 'Foundations in Faith' course that we held in the parish fired up church-going parishioners and they are still alight with the fire of faith. It was not addressed to beginners in the faith, but to long-term Catholics. They learnt about the very core of our faith in a way that was not academic and this was much easier to grasp for ordinary Catholics. The weekends on this course which were held in the parish centre, were wrapped in prayer, both by participants and by the whole parish, who were supporting it. All the participants declared that the discussions on faith matters in small groups and at meal times were the best part of the weekend, and for some it was the first time they had discussed the faith with fellow parishioners. This course developed a core group in the parish, who were able to *think catholic* and influence other parishioners. It helped to develop a catholic way of thinking, a catholic mentality amongst parishioners. Every church-going Catholic needs to be given the

---

[242] Rite of Christian Initiation for Adults – a course for adults entering the Church or seeking the faith

opportunity to know these foundations and to be encouraged to develop this Catholic mentality.

Developing a new system of adult faith learning

It must be pretty terrifying for the hierarchy of the Church to contemplate the mammoth task of setting up a system to educate the lay faithful so that it becomes the norm for parishes to be hubs of faith learning. But that it is not a good excuse for avoiding going down this track. As laity, we also need to accept the responsibility of exploring our faith to discover answers to our deep faith questions and realise that we are on a constant learning journey. We need to seek out and discover opportunities to delve into the real depths of our faith which are so rich, to enable us to develop a stronger relationship with Jesus.

It is interesting to note that during the Covid pandemic people felt the need to join online choirs and book clubs because they sought interaction and community. Many of these groupings continued on a face to face basis after the pandemic. The need for the sharing of ideas and interaction is part of our human make-up. We learn through community.

Folk often express their gratitude for the development of the University of the Third Age where all sorts of interests are catered for amongst retirees, but it always saddens me that this does not usually include Christianity. We do not have a University or even a Primary School of the Third Age (retirees) within the church, or even the Second age (the general working age population) or even the First age (young people). So we need to take a whole new look at how we deepen our relationship with Jesus by researching and learning about the riches of our faith. Then we need to learn techniques of how we pass on this grace-filled faith life to others, whether it be to family, friends, colleagues or seekers of the faith.

When there is a desire to go to university or college or learn a skilled trade, it is a requirement to read, research and study to gain the grades you need to deepen your knowledge of a proposed subject. Why is it so different in the Church? Why do people rarely consider researching their faith? We have people in our congregations who have skills, degrees and doctorates providing the background knowledge needed for their professional lives, yet it seems that the little faith knowledge you gain perhaps at school is enough to see you through 70/ 80 years of life without any further questioning. Are we doing the gift of faith an injustice?

Today we see endless programmes about researching our backgrounds, exploring our family tree to discover where we have come from, which shows clearly the need within people to discover their roots. Surely there should be a desire within us to research the roots of Christianity and discover its firm foundations. Changing the atmosphere in our parish communities so that faith discovery becomes a natural part of who we are as Catholics, would ensure and encourage parishioners to investigate the incredibly rich roots of our faith heritage and allow them to gain the confidence to pass it on.

Chapter 24

THE NEED TO TRAIN
ADULT LAY LEADERS

Where to begin this process

To make progress in the area of provision of adult faith education in our parishes we need to be realistic regarding the availability of leaders in this field. Parish priests have always been acknowledged as the experts in knowledge of the faith but their roles are changing. We need to recognize that parish priests are becoming ever busier as Churches and communities are amalgamated, so traditional ministerial duties take priority and the desire to provide programmes for adult faith learning in parishes moves further towards the distant horizon.

Certainly in the UK, and maybe in other places too, there are more retired priests who often act as supply cover or assist with weekend Masses in large parishes. Many of these experienced priests have great gifts and although they would not wish to take on the responsibility of another parish, with all that it entails, they still possess a desire to be involved in furthering the progress of God's kingdom. Their valuable expertise would be a huge asset to draw on in this field of adult education. It may be possible to set up a team structure where they could work alongside lay leaders helping to establish a system of modular learning for practising Catholics.

It is also evident that there is a lack of trained lay personnel to run these parish programmes, yet it is logical to believe that God has provided people who can fulfil this role with the skills needed for the growth of his Church and the development of God's kingdom. In Ephesians it says *'to some, his 'gift' was that they should be apostles; to some prophets; to some, evangelists; to some, pastors and teachers; to knit God's holy people together for the work of service to build up the Body of Christ'.*[243] Since God has gifted these skills to his children for the benefit of others, it is our responsibility to identify these skills and develop them constructively! It is important to note that at present we see many untrained catechists / lay leaders involved in teaching in parishes who feel they know enough about their faith and therefore do not feel the need to be trained. Through gentle persuasion and a parish or diocesan expectation of catechists to attend training, these catechists would soon discover the benefits of faith formation. On the other hand, many Catholics try to accompany people whom they wish to draw towards Christ and his Church, yet they feel they lack the skills.

Many early retired parishioners are eager to be involved in activities to assist the Church and could

---

[243] Eph 4:11-12

easily be trained to help their communities grow and develop in the faith. They would need to work within specified parameters after their training and need strong leadership to ensure they receive the necessary guidance to assist them in their specific role within the parish. Many lay people are only asked to help with the material and administrative running of the parish, and yet the spiritual upbuilding of the people is more important. To concentrate on keeping up the 'normal' Church functions while the Church itself is shrinking is folly. Laity have so many God-given skills that could be harnessed for the development of parish faith education hubs which could be accessible to all.

Adult faith education on multiple levels with trained guides

The Church needs to consider adult faith education on multiple levels: for those who have practised their faith throughout the years; for those rediscovering the faith after being estranged from it; and for those discovering the faith for the first time; and for parents who enrol their children on the sacramental programme, to name just a few. This type of adult faith education needs to be multi-faceted as people learn at different speeds and in different ways; some learn and gain the greatest benefit from guided discussion groups whilst others benefit more from individual study with a mentor.

Facilitating adults who have this yearning for a deeper knowledge of the faith should be a very natural core value of every parish. The first step would be for people to become immersed in an atmosphere of informal discovery of faith within a parish community. Parishes as faith education hubs, and the lifelong process of faith discovery is a new concept, and it will take time to become embedded in the normal practise of the faith life of Catholic adults. It is important to encourage Catholics (practising or not) to embark on this lifelong process where they will uncover new and exciting depths of the faith. The faith discovery (or rediscovery) train needs to be continually ongoing, repeating modules to make them easily accessible through all mediums, so that lifelong learning becomes the norm in our parishes. It is painful to see how much effort the Church invests in teaching children in reading, writing, maths, science and so on, and how little is invested in forming adults into the image of Christ. That was not Jesus' method of forming disciples.

Differing roles in Lay leadership

There are different strands within lay leadership in the field of faith education yet to be developed in the Church where training needs to be on good solid foundations. People who come forward to be trained will have varying skills and abilities, various amounts of available time and varying motivational levels to be considered. But generally there could be a structure developed within parishes where there is assistance from laity in faith education at progressive levels, beginning with **Accompaniers**, moving onto **Guides** and then **Catechists** (or leaders). Such training is good preparation for more than faith formation. Volunteers who have been through a process of deepening their faith would be more motivated to take on roles in other branches of Church life like youth ministry, liturgy and administration as well as in faith education.

Accompaniers

If we begin at the entry level of lay involvement in faith discovery we need to consider the concept of '**accompaniers**'. These are parishioners who learn the basic skills which will equip them to travel alongside people who are seeking answers to faith questions. Sometimes these questions are about life and not necessarily about faith, accompaniers would need to walk beside them and, when the opportunity arises, bring God into the conversations, and pray for them constantly. This will assist them in building a bridge of trust between them and God. Once people's interest in discovering more about the faith has been aroused, or they have had their initial questions answered, they can choose to delve further. This will enable them to discover whether this is what they believe, and if it is a way of life they wish to follow. Questions may also arise when someone returns to the faith after an absence, or even from someone who has faithfully practised their faith over the years. Those seeking answers maybe friends, family, or people within or re-joining the parish community.

Accompanying means being trained in how to listen as well as answering basic faith questions and welcoming folk into the community. As they gently befriend them, accompaniers would also encourage their participation in parish events, spiritual and social. Maintaining a sustained effort to keep in touch with people is essential as it creates a link or bridge with the Church whilst helping them to understand the faith and life in the worshipping community. Getting to know someone will help them to feel able to ask anything about the faith, but accompaniers may need to wait for a long time for the opportunity to witness and share the faith as they travel this journey together. If the number of non-believers drawn into the faith begins to grow, an ever expanding group of parishioners would need to be trained to be accompaniers.

Training accompaniers is something that Sherry Weddell has begun to develop through her Ananias course[244] at the St. Catherine of Sienna Institute in the States and which we were about to introduce in our parish. As stated in a previous chapter she feels it is essential to change the 'culture of silence' amongst Catholics which causes them to avoid sharing about their relationship with Jesus. She states:

'Being 'Ananias' for one another as we journey to follow Jesus can transform the culture of silence, replacing it with a culture in which a personal relationship with Jesus Christ and following him in the midst of his Church is normal. The fruit of a culture of discipleship is that more people are attracted to the community, and come to encounter Jesus themselves'.[245]

---

[244] S.A. Weddell *Ananias Course* at St. Catherine of Sienna Institute[online] Colorado Springs

[245] S.A. Weddell Ananias training at St. Catherine of Sienna Institute[online] Colorado Springs pg. 3

We must go a step further and encourage an atmosphere in which sharing about our relationship with Jesus amongst our fellow parishioners grows and becomes part of conversations throughout our natural interactions such as over tea/ coffee.

Accompaniers would also be invaluable to new parishioners who have newly arrived in the parish, or as personal contacts for parents seeking Baptism for their child, many of whom disappear after Baptism as no one talks to them in Church. These parents may have contact with the priest or a catechist, but rarely does anyone else greet them or even invite them for a coffee after Mass, let alone welcome them into the community and befriend them.

Guides

It is only after this process of accompaniment, that people will desire to access new levels of the faith and will be interested in the adult faith discovery train. In order for it to build up speed to move out of the station in the parish, some of the accompaniers would need to progress to become trained as **Guides** in order to lead faith discussion groups. We saw this developing when members of the Evangelisation Group led discussions with sacramental programme parents. Their confidence in doing this grew out of previously sharing in faith exploration.

This would highlight the need for guides to obtain a greater knowledge of theological aspects of the faith to enable them to provide input and to confidently lead discussion groups with a solid foundation of the faith. This depth of knowledge would give them a more secure basis to explain, for example, the Deposit of faith and how to begin to develop a relationship with Jesus, as well as a basic knowledge of salvation history. If different modules are to be available on the faith learning train, guides might need to take responsibility for delivering particular modules. It may be that a guide has a particular interest in a section of the faith, for example a great devotion to Mary, so maybe they could be trained in researching and delivering a module on Mary. Guides could also be involved in encouraging parishioners to participate in small well-led discussion groups, as well as helping in their organisation. They could take place in the parish facilities or in a home over a cup of coffee.

As leaders or facilitators of the discussion groups, guides would use their skills to pose significant questions to steer the group and would be responsible for enabling people to share and discuss without interruption from others. So often groups are derailed by a voice emerging with the familiar 'Oh yes, a similar thing happened to me' which then causes the discussion to go off at a totally unconnected tangent. These discussions are for those who have come to gain a greater understanding of a topic. If someone comes to sessions which are constantly derailed by tangential discussions, or leave having their questions unanswered, they may feel that their contribution is not valued and most likely they will not return. If, however, this situation can be turned around by an experienced guide, a process begins within those looking for answers. It allows them to open their hearts to faith discovery at a depth never experienced before and they begin to share a little more each time.

Catechists / leaders

Finally **Catechists**, or leaders of the faith learning programme, would need extra training in order to lead and promote courses and modules. They could be responsible for training accompaniers and guides to a certain agreed level, lead teams of laity within a parish and create new modules and courses in a set framework in collaboration with, and under the guidance of the parish priest. They would also need to ensure Safeguarding checks are in place and provide a support system for guides and accompaniers. Besides this they would need to keep a check that standards are continually reviewed and that teaching is in line with the Magisterium.

My research showed that many dioceses only provide a few training videos for catechists believing they are sufficient, yet Pope Francis felt the role is so important that in 2021 he instituted the Ministry of Catechists.[246] He created this ministry as a development of the thinking of the Council Fathers in the Second Vatican Council[247] and of Pope St Paul VI[248] who felt

---

[246] Pope Francis *Antiquum Ministerium* Motu Proprio (10 May 2021) [online]

[247] Pope Francis *Antiquum Ministerium* Motu Proprio (10 May 2021) No 4 quoting Ad Gentes 17 [online]

[248] Pope Francis *Antiquum Ministerium* Motu Proprio (10 May 2021) No 7 quoting Pope Paul VI in *Ministeria Quaedam* [online]

there were other ministries to be recognised besides readers and acolytes. But Pope Francis also stated his awareness that '*in our days, when there are so few clerics to evangelise such great multitudes and to carry out the pastoral ministry, the role of catechists is of the highest importance*'.[249]

The institution of the Ministry of Catechists was not to replace clerics but to assist them in the area of evangelisation and formation. Pope Francis was very clear that the skills of the catechist should be recognised as they work alongside clerics, when he stated that '*It is essential that they be faithful co-workers with priests and deacons, prepared to exercise their ministry wherever it may prove necessary, and motivated by true apostolic enthusiasm*'.[250]

Pope Francis insisted that catechists need to study their faith at a greater depth in order to pass on the faith when he stated that in order for them to be able to carry out their role with confidence, catechists must '*receive suitable biblical, theological, pastoral and pedagogical formation to be competent communicators of the truth of the faith*'.[251] He added

'*Every catechist must be a witness to the faith, a teacher and mystagogue, a companion and*

---

[249] Pope Francis *Antiquum Ministerium* Motu Proprio (10 May 2021) No 4 [online]

[250] Pope Francis *Antiquum Ministerium* Motu Proprio (10 May 2021 No 8 [online]

[251] Pope Francis *Antiquum Ministerium* Motu Proprio (10 May 2021) No 8 [online]

pedagogue, who teaches for the Church. Only through prayer, study, and direct participation in the life of the community can they grow in this identity and the integrity and responsibility that it entails, transmitting the faith as it develops through its different stages from the initial proclamation of the kerygma to the instruction that presents our new life in Christ and prepares for the sacraments of Christian initiation, and then to the ongoing formation that can allow each person to give an accounting of the hope within them'.[252]

Maybe raising the role of Catechist, to that of a ministry recognized by the Church, will encourage a growing desire in the Church hierarchy to follow the example of the one or two more discerning dioceses who now ask their catechists to undergo a 1 or 2 year training course and issue certificates of competence. There should also be an expectation that catechists participate in ongoing training. This in-depth look at the faith and appropriate training for parish lay leaders/ catechists, guides and accompaniers produces confident laity who are then able to work from solid foundations. Then they will be able to effectively guide others on the path of seeking more knowledge about the faith and the development of a deep relationship with Jesus. It would also lighten the load for many over worked parish priests and create effective teams of clerics and laity working together in the building of God's kingdom. In some cases, trained

---

[252] Pope Francis *Antiquum Ministerium* Motu Proprio (10 May 2021) No 6 [online]

lay catechists should be properly employed and must be treated as professionals in their field.

As part of the development of the Catechetical Institute at the Franciscan University at Steubenville, 2022 has seen the foundation of the International Guild of Catechists which hopes to connect Catechists around the world and give them access to online training.[253]

The art of listening

For those leading adult faith learning in parishes, it is essential that accompaniers, guides and catechists are trained to listen. The art of listening is much underrated, but it is important if we are to help people to progress in the faith. Pope Francis in Evangelii Gaudium 171 describes listening as *'an openness of heart which makes possible that closeness without which genuine spiritual encounter cannot occur'*. People who are exploring the faith need us to be more than merely bystanders, they need us to listen compassionately as they first unload their own baggage before they can begin to think in new ways. Often the stories they tell give an incredible insight of where they are coming from, and this can help to direct their future pathway in the faith. Evangelii Gaudium 171 goes on to state

'Only through such respectful and compassionate listening can we enter on the paths of true growth and awaken a yearning for the Christian ideal:

[253] Franciscan University of Stebenville – called ' Franciscan at home' [online] available at https://franciscanathome.com

the desire to respond fully to God's love, and to bring to fruition what he has sown in our lives'.

Catechists / Guides / Accompaniers, therefore, will also need to connect with individuals on a one-to-one basis to allow them to unload this baggage confidentially rather than in a group. Their training would give them the confidence to do this well and help the individual move forward in their faith search.

Training adult youth leaders

Here I would like to digress to share a little of what we learnt over the years by giving an example of how training adults before they launch into a programme of leadership is so important. This example shows the importance of a faith discovery journey as part of the preparation of leaders for our last youth group.

We always had youth groups in the parishes we served, and had great teams of leaders who gave so much; the kids had a great time, were safe off the streets and we tried to share our faith together. The value of this became evident when a young teenage girl died in the secondary school, and it was to the youth group that the teenagers turned for help in processing it within their faith and wanted time for prayer. Youth group members brought along their friends who were also struggling and they knew they would receive a warm welcome and help. But we learnt over the years that although these youth groups were good, they did not embed the children in faith, and leaders found it difficult to share their faith with the youth until we discovered *Lifeteen*[254] from The United States Conference of Catholic Bishops.

Lifeteen

Lifeteen was geared to having ***fun in the faith***. It began with six months of training for the leadership group, sharing our faith and delving into its roots, which led us to discover ways to help the young people relook at the practise of their faith. Once we began *Lifeteen* in our parish, these leaders walked alongside the youth to help them uncover the importance and mystery of faith which ran through our evenings and became an accepted element of our time with the youth. The leaders joined in everything from planning the sessions to participating in the games and creative sessions. They led discussions on faith and morals which were fun, and imparted knowledge as well as giving time for the youth to ask questions. They also took part in regular ongoing training sessions.

It was interesting that the older section of youth turned up for extra sessions to ask questions and discuss their faith as they felt listened to, and encouraged to confront their faith without being judged. We had youth Masses, which parishioners loved, and times of prayer led by the youth such as Stations of the Cross. During a youth night there would be prayer, fun and games together in a Christian manner, discussions and activities on a topic with the Catholic view point, and

---

[254] Lifeteen Catholic Youth Ministry *Leading Teens Closer to Christ* USCCB [online] https://lifeteen.com

food was always an essential part of the evening. Prayer and praise (with music) brought the evening to a close. Parents were invited to join us for this, they were intrigued and drawn into the prayer in increasing numbers. They kept returning as did the youth, many of whom continue to practise their faith today.

The point of this example was that leaders of any group within the parish need to first deepen their own faith and then to train and learn skills of how to walk alongside others on the pathway to Jesus. It was only when we trained the youth leaders and had ongoing training for them that they grew in confidence which enabled them to lead faith sharing sessions with the youth. These youth leaders from all walks of life were ready to continue to lead the youth when we left the parish. When a recently retired person was asked to help with the group they often said they did not know how to talk to young people, so we used to ask them 'if they could hula-hoop', in other words, 'could they have fun'. So many of them found they were naturals and the young people flocked round them.

Leaders responsible for the learning environment

To return to the idea of trained guides / catechists, it is important that they also receive training in planning and preparing well for a session. If people feel unwelcomed, uncomfortable and unsure of their surroundings and do not know what is about to happen in a session, levels of anxiety rise. If folk cannot hear the speaker properly or see the screen well, they mentally switch off. All of these things can prevent people from focusing on the topic at hand and all are preventable with a little forward planning.

Where discussions are organised, they should take place in a comfortable space, warm, airy, light and with decent facilities. Leaders need to check well in advance that the microphones work, the projector displays clear images and the room is set out well. Doing this at the last minute is like waiting for a disaster to happen, and it will! These things may seem obvious but I have so often seen disastrous sessions through lack of planning or preparation.

As participants arrive they need to be welcomed and made to feel at home, and a connection needs to be made by simple things, such as remembering their name and using it throughout the session.

Something which is often not in evidence as being considered to be important is that some privileged moments in accompanying will also happen on the hoof and need to be dealt with immediately. Faith leaders need to be trained to deal with and not to dismiss these often blessed but unexpected moments of sharing and growth in a person.

Structure of sessions

A further point to consider is that within an organised session which is part of a course, there needs to be a structure, a framework where one leads from one section onto the next so that there is a pattern established; this relaxes people as they know what is coming next. However, I do believe that, every once in a while, something extraordinary should happen. It wakes folk up, keeps them interested and it can also be fun.

A great example of this process was with Sacramental Programme parents who had been coming to discussion sessions where a pattern was established with an Alpha-type course where there was a hot meal, a talk and then discussion with prayer running through the evening. On a Saturday retreat with them, the morning followed the same pattern to help them settle. Then after a shared lunch they were asked to stand in groups and we played a simple game which got them laughing at how ridiculous it was, but it woke them up before the afternoon session which is often the hardest time for input.

Media usage

Parishes need to change and be brought into the 21st century which is one of the lessons which has emerged from the Covid pandemic. During this strange time, our ability to communicate through the media has greatly increased; grandparents have learnt how to Zoom, Skype or Tweet, and many teenage grandchildren have had frequent and deep conversations via media with older generations in the family that they would not normally have made time for. These together with all the other methods of media communication need to be rolled out and used well in our parishes. This would mean that catechists and guides would need to be familiar with all methods of communication via the media and training in this area may need to be provided for them. Each parish now needs to have an IT specialist to set up and maintain systems as well as helping others use these new methods of communication.

There is no doubt that face-to-face sessions and/or group discussions and personal interaction are so much more fruitful than Zoom discussions, but online contacts fill a gap and are preferred by some with incredibly busy lives. For example, if a parent on a Sacramental Programme is keen to take part, but is working the evening shift, surely they could catch up later or the next day via information provided on a website and a zoom session with the catechist or guide.

The Church cannot go back to how we existed before; it needs to incorporate new ways to reach the parents and young people today who live in world where media is as much part of their lives as brushing their teeth in the morning. The older generation are still running to catch up, but if encouraged, they can achieve this with some effort and training.

Learning through faith led activities

We also learn our faith by being drawn into a faith led activity and therefore Catechists need to think outside the box. They need to be creative, adventurous and willing to step out with new ideas to draw people in. For example for several years we had a team of parishioners, young mums and grandparents who gave retreat days for the primary school, both in the Church and parish centre, and in school. Activities were many and varied but were centred on scripture in word, action and song.

At the end of one of the retreat days at school all the children came together to present to parents the theme of Pentecost. For this we built a dove about six or seven feet long and wide with coat hangers and white cloth. Attached to it were streamers and the children brought it into the hall whilst telling the parents through song and action the meaning of Pentecost and the Holy Spirit. At a particular point I looked round at the parents and they were enthralled and, when it came time for the children to throw out the streamers (representing the gifts and graces of the Holy Spirit), the parents happily helped ensure they reached every part of the room and were delighted to be involved. They went out beaming and came to tell the team how they had learnt so much about Pentecost and enjoyed it as well. The light in their faces showed the truth of this, followed by an increased attendance at Church. So we learn by action and witness as well as deep thought and discussion. And it can be fun too!

Invite adults to share the richness of Church liturgies

It is also important for adults to be invited to experience the richness of other Church liturgies than Mass that perhaps they have not had access to, such as Exposition and Benediction and praying with one another. Catechists, guides and accompaniers could easily invite those they are walking alongside to come with them to Benediction or the rosary.

A clear example of the effect of this type of new experience came on the retreat day for parents mentioned in previous paragraphs which came to a conclusion with an explanation to help them to understand devotion to the Blessed Sacrament, and a description of what was about to happen. This was followed by a short time of Adoration before the Blessed Sacrament. We asked them to sit on their own in Church so that they would not be tempted to talk, and to turn off their phones and just to have time talking to God as a friend.

After about 10 minutes of silence they were invited to be prayed with by two or three of the leaders (who were terrified the first time we did this). One by one most (not all), went to ask for prayer, often about worries in family situations, or about the loss of a loved one and the grief experienced, or a hurt of some kind. They prayed for a few moments with the leaders. The whole service of Exposition only lasted about 30 minutes but the effect was profound. They were totally blown away as it was something they had never experienced and had never been taught about, yet it was so simple. We found after this that several of the parents were trying to find times to pray at home in silence for a few minutes several times in the week.

Synodality

It is important for concerned Catholics to keep updated with what is happening within the Church today, as well as knowing what happened in the past and to learn about these things through the Church rather than the secular media. This applies especially to leaders such as catechists, guides and accompaniers. In the past the Church's progress was rarely questioned by parishioners, but now as adult faith formation develops for congregants, it should facilitate greater participation in the development of the Church. The Church is a living, developing entity which enables it to deal with new problems in each age, and worshippers need access to information regularly to ensure they feel part of the Church's growth and development.

The main topic of discussion in our Church today is the meaning of Synodality. What does it mean for the average person? It is explained simply by Pope Francis when he spoke about the Amazonian Synod in Austen Ivereigh's book '*Let us dream*'.[255] He spoke about the scenario where those who come together to discuss within the Church often come with their own agendas or pet theories. For example, people often attend meetings with a personal agenda such as 'this is what I want from this meeting - a decision on this'. If this does not happen, they often feel the meeting was a waste of time. If, however, we come with an open heart and listen to what others say, put our point of view, yes, but then spend time listening to the Holy Spirit, often there is consensus of opinion. This frequently goes along a new track that no-one had thought of, but it often solves many

---

[255] A. Invereigh *Let us Dream: The Path to a Better Future; in conversation with Pope Francis* (London: Simon & Schuster UK Ltd 2020) pp. 89-90, 91-94

difficulties – Pope Francis calls this '*overflow*'[256] and it is often the right way forward.

How does this affect me?

We need to ask ourselves some questions if we are to understand Synodality. When attending a discussion group, am I the person who comes with an agenda, and want my issues to be discussed? Or am I the one who sits quietly and says nothing, as I can't get a word in because someone is hogging the floor about a particular issue? How different that meeting would be if all prayed for the Holy Spirit to come upon the group and to speak through his people. It would involve listening to one another and not coming with a set agenda, but coming with a willingness to follow the Holy Spirit however he would lead.

In a recent online discussion group we were asked to consider the role of the Holy Spirit in our parish activities. I listened to the other members of the group for a while. These were good people who do so much in their parishes. But then I posed the question 'when do we stop and ask the Holy Spirit for his guidance?' The response was 'yes, we know all about that, but something practical needs doing and this is what we could do'. So the Holy Spirit was dismissed as irrelevant. Maybe now, as preparation takes place throughout the world for the Synod on Synodality, it is

---

[256] A. Invereigh *Let us Dream: The Path to a Better Future; in conversation with Pope Francis* (London: Simon & Schuster UK Ltd 2020) pp. 80 ff

time for priests and laity alike to stop, and come before the Lord and ask the Holy Spirit to speak to our hearts, and the hearts of our communities. Then we will need to listen to discover if he is saying a similar message in many hearts so that we, the Church, can move forward along the same track - his track not ours.

To summarise

Several themes have emerged in these writings including the concept of lifelong faith learning becoming the norm in our parishes, and discovering our faith heritage whilst developing an ever deepening relationship with Jesus. The whole subject is a huge canyon to be crossed in new and unchartered territory. The Church has a massive job in tackling this development of a universal process of adult faith learning. It means that we need to start small in a diocese, so that they can develop parishes as local central hubs for adult faith learning. It is important that this learning be embedded in parish communities rather than some outside agency, as the parish is the basic building block of the Church. Starting small would help to solve the constant problem in parishes of there never being enough volunteers. We discovered that concentrating on training a particular group, who then went on to train others, widened the circle of committed volunteers.

In discussions with many Catholics, laity and clergy, we have discovered people who have become disenchanted with the Church, not only through loss of trust in it, but also through feeling side-lined as their God given skills are unused. We need, therefore to discover ways to utilise these skills according to the Lord's plan to build up the Church, and cease dismissing new and unusual ideas. Our prayer for the Church is that it becomes a listening Church, one that is not afraid to use all the skills within it, to share the burden of spreading the Good News with well-formed capable members who are eager to listen to, and to follow the Holy Spirit.

This ever growing need for the local church, the parish, to assist adults in developing their knowledge and love for their faith and the Church is becoming more and more important as we live in a culture that is happy to incessantly berate others and pursue only what will benefit the individual, which creates a toxic atmosphere. If the generations of the future are to live in a Christian world that cares for one another, they need to understand their Christian roots. It is, therefore, this generation's responsibility to find a way to open the doors to encourage people to follow the pathway of faith discovery which is a lifelong journey.

Our youth group put it very eloquently when asked 'what would their life be like if Jesus had not lived on this earth? They began to think and suddenly realised we would not have Easter nor Christmas. When asked how they felt about it, they thought it was awful not just because they would not receive Easter eggs or Christmas presents, they went onto say 'we would not know how to live and how to treat each other.

However much people reject Christianity, it is the firm foundation of society. We just need to follow Jesus as he shows us how to open the eyes of the world to the pivotal reality that He is the only true way to the Father.

Dear Reader

If this book has helped you to stop and think, we would love to hear your reflections. We are always grateful for the chance to share thoughts with others who are concerned with the spiritual life and the future of the Church.

Please contact us by : -

Email - hopefulcatholics@gmail.com
Blog / Web – hopefulcatholics.com
Facebook – Hopeful Catholics

If you are interested in discussing how people in your parish could benefit from hearing about the themes in this book, please contact us.

Thankyou for reading it.

God bless
Fr. Brian and Anne

BIBLIOGRAPHY

Scripture
The Holy Bible Jerusalem Study version (1966)

Magisterial Documents
Holy See, *Catechism of the Catholic Church,* London Geoffrey Chapman, A Cassell imprint 1945
Holy See, *Directory for Catechesis, London.* Catholic Truth Society 2020

Online Holy See
Clement Pope (before 70 AD) *First Letter to the Corinthians* [online] Rome. Holy See
Available on the World Wide Web [3 November 2022]
https://www.newadvent.org/fathers/1010.htm

Francis Pope (2021) *Antiquum Ministerium* [online]. Rome. Holy See
Available on the World Wide Web
https://www.vatican.va/content/francesco/en/motu_ proprio/documents/papa-francesco-motu-proprio-20210510_antiquum-ministerium.html [2 December 2021]

Francis Pope (2020) *Querida Amazonia* [online]. Rome. Holy See
Available on the World Wide Web
https://www.vatican.va/content/francesco/en/apost_exhortations/documents/papa-francesco_esortazione-ap_20200202_querida-amazonia.html [2 December 2021]

John Paul II Pope St, (1988) *Christifideles Laici* [online]. Rome. Holy See
Available on the World Wide Web
https://www.vatican.va/content/john-paul-ii/en/apost_exhortations/documents/hf_jp-ii_exh_30121988_christifideles-laici.html [2 December 2021]

John Paul II Pope St, (1990) *Redemptoris Missio* [online]. Rome. Holy See
Available on the World Wide Web
https://www.vatican.va/content/john-paul-ii/en/encyclicals/documents/hf_jp-ii_enc_07121990_redemptoris-missio.html [2 December 2021]

John Paul II Pope St, (23 May 2004) *38th World Communications Day Message* [online]. Rome. Holy See
Available on the World Wide Web
https://www.vatican.va/content/john-paul-ii/en/messages/communications/documents/hf_jp-ii_mes_20040124_world-communications-day.html [2 December 2021]

Paul VI, Pope St, (1975) *Evangelii Nuntiandi* [online].
Rome. Holy See
Available on the World Wide Web
https://www.vatican.va/content/paul-vi/en/apost_
exhortations/documents/hf_p-vi_exh_19751208_
evangelii-nuntiandi.html [2 December 2021]

Paul VI, Pope ST, (1964) *Lumen Gentium* [online].
Rome. Holy See
Available on the World Wide Web
Lumen gentium (vatican.va)
https://www.vatican.va/archive/hist_councils/ii_
vatican_council/documents/vat-ii_const_19641121_
lumen-gentium_en.html [2 December 2021]

Paul VI, Paul Pope St, (1979) *Redemptor Hominis*
[online]. Rome. Holy See
Available on the World Wide Web
https://www.vatican.va/content/john-paul-ii/en/
encyclicals/documents/hf_jp-ii_enc_04031979_
redemptor-hominis.html [2 December 2021]

<u>Books</u>
Butcher C A *The Cloud of Unknowing (with the Book
of Privy Counsel)* (Boston & London: Shambhala
Publications, Inc.2009)

Invereigh A. *Let us Dream: The Path to a Better
Future; in conversation with Pope Francis* (London:
Simon & Schuster UK Ltd 2020)

Mallon J. Fr, Divine *Renovation* (Toronto: Novalis 2016)

Maryvale Institute *Echoes: Echoing Christ* (London: The Catholic Truth Society 2012)

Newman J.H. *Lectures on the Present Position of Catholics (Works of Cardinal John Henry Newman: The Birmingham Oratory Millennium Edition S.)* (Leominister: Gracewing, 2000)

Weddell S A. *Forming Intentional Disciples: The Path to Knowing and Following Jesus* (Huntington: Our Sunday Visitor Publications Division, 2012)

Online
Barron Bishop Word *on Fire Series: Proclaiming Christ in the Culture* [online]
Available on the World Wide Web
https://www.wordonfire.org

Benedict XVI Pope & Winstel Tobias "War Ich ein guter Seelsorger?"in *Herder Korrespondenz* (August 2021)
Available on the World Wide Web
https://www.herder.de/unternehmen/verlage/verlag-herder/ ; https://pdfcoffee.com/herder-korrespondenz-war-ich-ein-guter-seelsorger-pdf-free.html

Catherine of Siena. St, *Oimere Institute of Mystical Experience Research and Education* [online]
Quoting Carol Lee Flinders in *A Little Book of Women Mystics*
Originally in *The Letters of Catherine of Siena* (4 vols), Letter T137.
Available on the World Wide Web
https://imere.org/third-party-story/mystical-experience-saint-catherine-siena/

Campion E. St, (1781) *Challenge to the Privy Council (Campion's "Brag")* [online] Catholic answers 1994 Catholic cutlure.org
Available on the World Wide Web
https://www.catholicculture.org/commentary/st-edmund-campion-campions-brag/

Christlife Ministries *Catholic Ministry for Evangelisation*
Available on the World Wide Web
ChristLife | Catholic Ministry for Evangelization
https://christlife.org/
Franciscan University of Steubenville Catechetical Institute – called 'Franciscan at home'
Available on the World Wide Web
https://franciscanathome.com
Fry C., The Sleep of Prisoners,
Available on the World Wide Web
https://Grateful.org/resource/A-Sleep-of-Prisoners

Graves D., Julian of Norwich St. Revelations of Divine Love, 13th Showing D, 1342-1416 in Christian *History Institute*, Article No. 31. [2 December2021]
Available on the World Wide Web
https://christianhistoryinstitute.org/incontext/article/julian

Guareschi G., (1954) *The Ugly Maddona* in Don Camillos' Dilemma *Wordpress* [online] (2017)
Available on the World Wide Web
https://sixtogarcia.wordpress.com/2017/02/18/the-ugly-maddonna-don-camillos-dilemma/

Hopkins G.M. *God's Grandeur* in *Gerard Manley Hopkins:Poems and Prose* (Penguin Classics, 1985)
Available on the World Wide Web
God's Grandeur by Gerard Manley Hopkins | Poetry Foundation
https://www.poetry/foundation.org/poems/44395/god's grandeur

Hopkins G.M. *Spring and Fall* in *Gerard Manley Hopkins: Poems and Prose* (Penguin Classics, 1985)
Available on the World Wide Web
Spring and Fall by Gerard Manley Hopkins | Poetry Foundation
https://www.poetryfoundation.org/poems/44400/spring-and-fall

Iannicelli M &J. Bible Timeline Course [online]
Available on the World Wide Web
https://www.comeandsee.org

Lawrence, D. H. (1916) *Amores.* [online] New York: B. W. Huebsch, 1916; Bartleby.com, 1999.
Available on the World Wide Web
www.bartleby.com/127/

Lifeteen Catholic Youth Ministry *Leading Teens Closer to Christ* USCCB [online]
Available on the World Wide Web
https://lifeteen.com

Newman J. H. *Cor ad cor loquitur* The International Centre of Newman Friends
Available on the World Wide Web
"Cor ad cor loquitur" John Henry Cardinal Newman's Coat of Arms - The International Centre of Newman Friends (newmanfriendsinternational.org)

Spadaro, A. (SJ) *A Big Heart Open to God: An interview with Pope Francis* America the Jesuit Review (2013) [online]
Available on the World Wide Web
https://www.americamagazine.org/faith/2013/09/30/big-heart-open-God-interview-pope-francis

Wang S. Fr, (2021) *Sycamore: The Catholic Faith Explained* [online]
Available on the World Wide Web
https://www.sycamore.fm

Weddell S.A. *Ananias Course* at St. Catherine of Sienna Institute [online] Colorado Springs
Available on the World Wide Web
https://siena.org

9 781803 813905